Little Eden

Also by Eva Figes

Fiction

EQUINOX

WINTER JOURNEY

KONEK LANDING

B

DAYS

NELLY'S VISION

WAKING

LIGHT

THE SEVEN AGES

Non-fiction

PATRIARCHAL ATTITUDES

TRAGEDY AND SOCIAL EVOLUTION

SEX AND SUBTERFUGE

Little Eden
A CHILD AT WAR

EVA FIGES

Persea Books
New York

Persea Books
225 Lafayette Street
New York, New York 10012

Library of Congress Cataloging-in-Publication Data

Figes, Eva.
Little Eden.

Reprint. Originally published: London ; Boston :
Faber and Faber, 1978.
1. Figes, Eva—Biography—Youth. 2. Novelists,
English—20th century—Biography. 3. Refugees,
Jewish—Great Britain—Biography. I. Title.
PR6056.I46Z468   1987   823'.914   [B]   87-2398
ISBN 0-89255-121-6

Printed in the United States of America

First U.S. Edition

Little Eden

I

I DO NOT know why I never went back before. I saw it marked up on a signpost at odd times over the years, unexpectedly, and each time I was tempted to change my plans for the day and go there instead. But I do not drive a car, and as a passenger I was always whisked off in the wrong direction, unable to explain adequately, or in time, why I wanted to go somewhere else on impulse. Once, crammed in a minibus full of youngish authors and poets, on our way to a lunch date from Cheltenham, I suddenly recognised the curve of the lane along which we were speeding. I had not been taking much notice of our route when I glanced out of the window and exclaimed 'I know this place' before I could even put a name to it, the high trees and the old iron gate followed by open fields on the left, the low stone wall enclosing the wooded grounds to the right. Like driving into a dream, and even while you dream saying, I have dreamed this place before, I found myself knowing each tree and blade of grass: the massive old beech tree in the middle of the field to my left, an island of shade or shelter, the fringe of woodland on the horizon, the slope of the land and the way the lane would curve, following the old stone wall, until we came to the junction with the London road. I knew one had to turn left for London, and right to reach the centre of the town. But we drove straight on for our lunch appointment, already late, whilst I craned my head to catch a glimpse of my childhood, buried by years but not forgotten, lost, and now suddenly found.

That was ten years ago, but since then the image of myself speeding along that stretch of unchanged road has recurred like a haunting snatch of melody. Having, by a minor miracle,

found myself suddenly back in the past, in a landscape unchanged, frozen in time nearly thirty years later, I travelled
down it often now, between sleeping and waking, or in day-
dreaming intervals, walked down the muddy avenue of high
trees shedding their leaves underfoot, heard the creak of the
iron gate as we came into Grove Lane. My brother and I had
once taken a delight in shuffling through a pile of autumn leaves
which the roadsweeper had only just swept to one side, scatter-
ing them anew, while my mother protested at our antisocial
high spirits. I was lucky to have found it just in time. When I
finally did go back the narrow lane had become a dual carriageway and the old iron gate had gone.

My sense of continuity was strengthened by another small
coincidence which stuck in my mind. That the subject should
have come up at all during such a necessarily brief conversation
was odd, and should have told me something. But what struck
me, and what I remembered afterwards, long after the organiser had dropped me at Oxford station and thanked me for my
lecture, was the fact that he had taught at the local grammar
school, knew the family on the farm and had taught Jack, the
farmer's son. What was more, he thought the family still ran the
farm. I stored that bit of information in my head and, after
another few years, acted on it. The ex-teacher from the Department of Education and Science was right: Jack answered my
letter.

But long before I acted on it, I kept remembering his words
as he dropped me at the station: 'To think of you walking up
and down the Whiteway as a small child all those years ago—
from now on I shall think of you like that.' I saw myself trailing
the long weary length of that road without a turning as dusk
was falling, stopping with aching legs to search for small
diversions in hedgerow or ditch—berries, rosehips, a feather
caught in the tangle of thorn. It was late in the year and there
were few wild flowers left to find. A long road, a boring road for
small children trudging home with the mists of winter closing
in, and the fact that it had cut through the countryside into
the mists of prehistory long before the Romans came and left,
that carts had trundled and men had stumbled through puddles

and ruts which froze in winter long before, taking the same direction across this stretch of flat land, was unknown to us. We began to cheer up only when we saw the gateway to the farm, the outline of barn and outhouses through the avenue of trees, because it meant we were nearly home.

The long hedgerow and the flat field beyond it have gone, swallowed up by a new housing estate. The town has grown since the war. Windows of neat surburban postwar prosperity look across the old orchard wall to where, through the trees, the old Cotswold stone farmhouse with its high chimneys is still visible through the trees.

Jack had answered my letter. Yes, he had taken over from his father many years ago. Why did I not pay them a call? I walked through the gateway and under the quiet old trees almost on tiptoe, holding my breath in the hushed excitement of a moment I wanted to savour for as long as possible, as I recognised each branch, tree, puddle, gate, shadows and smells, walls and outhouses. On this peaceful afternoon of early summer I could not believe my luck. I had walked into a sanctuary of the past as though into a church, and I responded to the atmosphere of what was for me, just then, a holy place.

2

1940. It had been a hot, fine summer. In March 1939 we had found a small flat in north-west London, a jerry-built mock medieval castle on the slope of a hill, surrounded by semi-detached houses and more fanciful examples of the housing developer's art—some classy looking thatched cottages and two more apartment blocks decked out as castles, including turrets, crenellated roofs, and narrow slit windows from which one could take potshots at invaders.

The whole area was unfinished, a new suburban development where plans had been left unfinished at the outbreak of war, leaving patches of waste ground, several genuine cottages which had to be propped up to stop them falling down, the bare iron girders of a new school where work had suddenly stopped, and several acres of fields which were still put to agricultural use. There were muddy lanes, too, which had existed long before London reached out this far, and provided a short cut for children going to school. Bacon Lane, enclosed by high hedgerows, wound between the field which contained the new municipal swimming pool, which had been finished before war broke out, and the field in which stood the massive girders of the planned school, which had not. Behind the swimming pool the corn was stooked late in that hot dry summer, and we played hide and seek in the dry brittle stuff, the dust getting into our noses, within earshot of the buses and lorries on the main road nearby. We picnicked under a line of ancient oaks, running wild in a meadow which should have been turned into a municipal park and would later be dug up for allotments. Small market gardens still flourished in spite of the traffic on the main road and the new gas company showroom, and further out, towards Barn Hill, you could still meet the odd cow grazing and climb stiles from one steep field to the next.

1940 was a summer of clear blue skies, and we spent a lot of our time staring up into it, trying to identify planes. My brother was only six, but already a lot of male kudos was attached to his ability to identify a Spitfire or Hurricane by the shape of the wings. He felt thoroughly put down when he got it wrong, or so the man sitting on the same bench under the line of old oak trees told him. Once, coming back up the hill from the swimming pool with damp towels rolled round our swimsuits, we were lucky enough to see a dogfight right over our heads. Three of us stood gawping, heads craned back, as the two planes wheeled and whined and sent out little puffs of white smoke into the clear blue, until a door opened on the other side of the road and a man yelled: 'Oi—what the hell do you kids think you're doing? Come in here at once.' And he made us stand in his hallway until the sounds had died away, and the fun was over.

They were exciting at first, those daylight raids. Not much really seemed to happen in our outlying suburb, nothing serious. When the sirens howled we were kept indoors and, unable to watch the sky, listened intently for telltale engine noises which were also part of the latest craze, plane-spotting. A steady drone meant it was 'one of ours', but German engines produced an intermittent, hiccupping sort of noise, and our aural identification of a Jerry plane overhead was usually confirmed by a loud explosion as it dropped a bomb, or the sound of gunfire.

But one night the game got out of control. The noise outside was unlike anything I had ever heard: it seemed to be coming from all directions at once, and in the darkness the whole world shook. My mother got me out of bed, made reassuring noises as the walls shook and the deafening thunder continued, took us both into the hallway for fear of flying glass. I assured her that I was not in the least bit frightened. Then I suddenly went into the bathroom and, to my own astonishment, vomited quite unexpectedly into the washbasin.

* * *

It must have been about this time that Zoë and Hillie decided that a town on the south coast was no place to go on running a school for small children, packed their belongings, and moved inland from Leigh-on-Sea to a safe reception area. In the archives I found their first advertisement in the local newspaper, dated June 15th 1940:

> LEIGH HEATH SCHOOL, Arkenside,
> Lewis-lane, Cirencester; Kindergarten
> School; vacancies for boarders and day
> pupils.—Apply: Principals.

And on September 28th of that year, to coincide with our arrival from London, the *Gloucestershire and Wiltshire Standard* carried another advertisement, which read: Arkenside Preparatory and Kindergarten School, Lewislane, Cirencester, have vacancies for Officers' Children.

My father was a mere private in the Pioneer Corps, but the sisters were happy to accept us as pupils since, as refugees from Nazi Germany, we could not be categorised socially in the normal way. They saw at once that my mother was 'a lady', and said so. Anyhow, most of the German Jews who had managed to get into England before the outbreak of war came from a superior social background. The immigration procedures had been very strict. Whatever their normal prejudices, the English middle class found it easy to feel sorry for refugees whose manners and clothing betrayed a style of living equal or superior to their own, even if they were Jews and had now fallen on hard times.

The tone of the advertisement sounds odd now, when ability to pay has become the only criterion. But if the Misses Sargent shared social attitudes of their type at that time, there was nothing abnormal about their advertisement, and it was in no way outrageously snobbish for 1940. Ladies advertising for housemaids or cooks general in the columns of the same newspaper (and they were still doing so with great regularity) would refer to themselves as officers' wives if the number of staff kept sounded unimpressive, small enough to call their social status into question.

As for the two sisters, they had been firmly moulded in early childhood and were conscious of carrying on a tradition handed down to them by their respectable parents. As their pupils, they inculcated us with old-fashioned manners which did us no harm. It was drummed into us how fortunate we were to have the chance to benefit from this tradition, and that it behoved us as standard-bearers of better breeding and education not to let the side down. Arkenside was a large semi-detached Victorian villa across the road from the grim overcrowded council school then still housed in the building originally erected by the Board of Guardians after the 1870 Education Act. The noise from across the road when school was out sounded almost frightening in our spacious house with its quiet rooms and large garden. From our first-floor landing we could see the noisy rabble milling round the asphalt playground surrounded by dismal prison walls, or flooding on to the pavements when they were released at the end of the day, and we viewed them with a mixture of pity and alarm. Hillie told us how lucky we were in comparison, as we looked down at them and listened to the unruly noise. But we were frightened of them, rather like small Marie-Antoinettes watching the mob from our palace windows.

I think we must have been encouraged to see ourselves as different, every hour of the day. Only a short time before, at school in London, I had been part of just such a wild council school mob myself, and had come to accept it as normal.

*　*　*

In London, for the past year, apart from a few weeks in Scotland waiting for a German invasion which never came, I had been trying very hard to get myself accepted in the childhood network of streets, school and playground whose laws were strange to me. I was foreign, used to large households with servants. All my life I had been sheltered, not only from the realities of poverty, but from the much harsher realities of life in Germany. As a small child I did not look particularly Jewish, and I could not have told you what the word meant. The adult world was wrapped in mysteries, sensed tension not understood, but always I was cushioned from the impact

13

of harsh reality. My father had been arrested while on a business trip to Düsseldorf, so his continued absence was easily explained. He was simply 'away' on business. My nursemaid, who later died of cholera in a concentration camp, organised a singsong in a back room away from the street while the smashing and looting, the beating and killing, went on four floors below at street level. All the servants had instructions to lie, and they must have been quite good at it. My nursemaid only got caught out once: when I stopped outside a shop displaying brown uniforms and leather belts and boots, and asked what they were for. She did not answer, she had no answer ready, which is why I remember that shop so vividly. But the smashed shop windows did not make much impression, because my question was promptly answered by prearrangement: they are being repaired. My brother and I could see that the shops were being repaired, so the aftermath of the *Kristallnacht* faded into everyday reality.

But our sheltered and comfortable existence ended the day my father came back from concentration camp. From that moment on I felt caught up in a drama, which started with the housemaid Edith waiting for us on the pavement in her black and white uniform. We got off the tram with the nursemaid and I saw her standing outside the main house door, without even a coat slung over her shoulders. The nurse was told not to bring us indoors, but to take us straight on to our grandparents. Herr Unger had scarlet fever.

We spent some time with my grandparents, where I slept on a sofa and we had English lessons in the afternoons from a young German woman and learnt a few words and phrases which later proved quite useless. After a while my grandparents, who only had a small flat and one servant, were given a rest, and we were moved to my other, widowed grandmother, who lived in gloomy and palatial splendour in a vast apartment on the Kurfürstendamm. Here I caught only a brief glimpse of my mother, who turned up to settle a row which had flared up between my grandmother and the nurse, whose nerves appeared to have reached breaking point.

The day we were finally brought back home was also memorable. My father stood in the living room, looking pale

14

and thin. But we knew he had been ill. What I had not been led to expect was the state of the apartment: the living room was almost bare of furniture, and the carpets had disappeared. My father grinned at my puzzled astonishment on seeing familiar surroundings so changed.

'We're going to England,' he said, and our excitement changed to terror when we made too much noise at the passport office and a man in military uniform with a swastika armband frightened us into round-eyed silence when he shouted at us to keep quiet and glared down at us from his desk while he examined the passports. And when we went to the British Embassy my father only had to warn us once: we waited in the old-fashioned hallway in subdued awe, quiet as mice. By now, aged six, I had learned that officialdom was to be feared, understood that bureaucrats exercised powers of life and death over people and, judging by the Nazi at the passport office, they could exercise it arbitrarily, depending on their mood and how you behaved.

Crowded into two cars, accompanied by two grandmothers, my grandfather, and an aunt, we drove in a rather sombre mood, like a funeral cortège, to the airport at Tempelhof. It was a bleak, overcast day. During the customs formalities it began to hail and I saw my grandfather outside the plate glass windows peering in to try and catch a final glimpse of us. He looked very forlorn outside, with the hailstones coming down on him, though he did not seem to notice them. He had not seen me: I pulled at the bottom of my father's coat to draw his attention but he was much too busy to take any notice. Afterwards, settled in the aeroplane, they were only a remote group of tiny figures standing outside the building, waiting for the plane to take off. We were told to wave, but I do not suppose they even saw us.

My brother, aged four, caused a last-minute diversion by announcing in a loud voice that, contrary to instructions, he had not spent his pocket money. He had it on him. He knew that from now on we would be poor, so if father ran short of cash he could rely on him to help out. The whole plane smiled at the pudgy small boy with ash blond hair who thought himself a

15

responsible man with just over one mark in his pocket, but my mother's smile was strained and anxious. I had been taken into a small shop a few days earlier and instructed to spend my money on anything, whether I wanted it or not, but my brother's childhood instinct for hoarding money had more than a touch of high drama on this occasion. He felt self-important and spoke in a very loud voice. By now I knew enough to be anxious in case we were all taken off the plane at the last minute.

But we took off, leaving everything behind. For years I was to take off, in a recurring dream, leaving them all behind, under that dark menacing sky.

My father had depicted England as the promised land with its own mythology: policemen with funny helmets, a city of buildings streaked black and white, regularly enveloped in dense fogs of legendary oddness, old railway stations where the taxis came right inside the station. Reality became, first a sordid boarding-house off the Finchley Road where I was scared to go to sleep at nights, then a small surburban flat where the furniture which we had brought from Berlin would not fit. Large Persian carpets lay rolled up against the wall as they were far too long for the small floors, sideboards and wardrobes and beds took up so much space that there was no room left to move. We rapidly acquired a new mythology of England: small rooms, draughty windows without double glazing, no central heating, outside plumbing which froze and started an indoor flood at the first sign of winter, and open coal fires which scorched your face whilst your back remained icy.

I started school, and my difficulties began. They did not really resolve themselves until I passed the eleven-plus and moved on to the local grammar school, but the period of fifteen months I spent in Cirencester was a welcome respite from the private war in which I found myself involved for so many years, no doubt one reason why it turned out to be such a special time.

When I came to Cirencester in 1940 I was raw with the effort of a year in which I had tried, oh so hard, to acclimatise not just to a foreign country in language and geography. If I had moved to Mayfair or Kensington I doubt whether I would have noticed any change. The foreign country was made up of a network of small, jerry-built semi-detached houses where children ran loose in the quiet residential streets, uncontrolled by adults. Nursemaids were unheard of, mothers did their own housework and allowed their children out of doors until dark: to fight, climb trees, invent dangerous games, sneak into back gardens for missing balls, roam from street to street and house to house until dusk or hunger drove us home. To my amazement my mother, who now did her own housework, allowed me to run wild and asked no questions. It was as though that other world of supervised walks, decorum and curtsies, separate meals in the day nursery, had been totally negated, by more than mere absence of money.

I liked being poor. I saw much more of my mother, and playing with gangs of children in the streets was exciting, an endless adventure. But I suffered from a handicap: from the day I was introduced into a classroom of forty staring children in my odd foreign clothes, only able to speak a few words, writing a peculiar script which my teacher dismissed as scribble, I was branded. I was allowed to join in girls' games on sufferance, and made to feel excluded from more secret rites. Even though I quickly learned the language and the tribal customs of alley and playground, the fact that I had arrived as a foreign child was never forgotten or forgiven, and with the rise of anti-German feeling after the outbreak of war my nationality was always good for abuse. The girls were the worst: they mostly played in groups, and my acceptance seemed to depend entirely on the mood of the acknowledged leader, whose hostility immediately infected the others. My troubles were offset but perhaps also exacerbated by the fact that as a shy, withdrawn little foreigner I quickly became the object of chivalrous attention from several small boys in the class, who invited me to tea, brought me flowers from their back garden, and came to call for me on their way to school. My popularity with boys only made the girls more standoffish and hostile, since they were openly jealous.

I learned to hate that school anyhow, for its crass teaching methods, but I was never to live down my German origin there, long after my English was perfect and I could conform to the patterns of the playground with the rest. I never knew when I would be accused next of being one of the hated enemy, except that I knew I would be. I was conscious of injustice, since my father was a soldier in the British army, which was more than most of their fathers were. But somehow these things were never open to discussion. I was too hurt and confused, my accusers too confident in their self-righteous prejudice.

Perhaps I suffered no more than any intelligent and sensitive child in such a group, but this particular group always had a stick to beat me with, and I never knew when they would take it into their heads to turn on me. At the dinner table 'shiny' spoons were much sought after as a status symbol. As a mark of friendship girls would go and get one for their friends from the cutlery tray. Nobody ever offered to find one for me. Conscious of a slight, I acquired one of the rare shiny spoons and took to keeping it in my purse, ready for the next day's meal. A few days later I found a gang of girls waiting for me as I came out of school. As usual there was a leader. They accused me of stealing cutlery and made me open my purse. I was marched off to one of the 'dinner ladies', who not only would not listen to my explanation, but dismissed me with the words: 'No English child would ever do a thing like that.' I tried to keep my head high, the tears back, as I walked home, followed by the jeers and catcalls of my classmates.

By next morning those girls were friendly once more, treated me as though nothing had happened. It was just one of those things, part of the fun and games of everyday life, and perhaps they had already forgotten the incident. But I never forgot it. Unfortunately I was proud as well as an enemy alien, and in later years I took to spending a lot of my free time in the home for parentless German-Jewish children next door to the school, where I could feel accepted as part of a strongly bonded group. Although I knew I was lucky in comparison to these children, I sometimes envied them for being all together under one large roof. It was fun there, like a permanent holiday camp, and the youth leaders always accepted me and made me welcome, when

I came to join in their games. They lived openly and proudly, whilst my family was trying to hide, become English, or at least merge into the background and avoid giving any possible offence to English neighbours. Rule one: never speak German.

But in the summer of 1940 my private war was still intermittent. I had a lot of fun, climbing trees, playing cowboys and Indians, learning to chant, with appropriate actions:

Underneath the spreading chestnut tree
Mister Chamberlain said to me:
If you want to get your gasmask free,
Join the blinking A.R.P.

Of course gasmasks were distributed free anyhow. We had been fitted out, along with a queue of other people, in the front room of a semi-detached house stacked high with brown cardboard boxes. They caused a lot of hilarity at school when we had gasmask drill, giggling at each other in our weird rubber muzzles. We then had to march, or rather, stumble, in disorderly file down the long corridors to the school cloakrooms, which had been reinforced to double as air raid shelters. It was hard going, since we could not see our feet and the celluloid window steamed up almost immediately. It was hot, and smelt funny, of rubber, and breathing was hard, suffocating work. We would have liked the Mickey Mouse masks, but these were only issued to very young children, who were much admired and envied in consequence.

During the short summer of 1939 there had been several excited reunions with friends or relatives who had managed to get out of Germany. My father's older sister arrived, minus her luggage. A family with two sons, with whom I used to play in the old days, came to visit us on their way to the States. All this stopped with the outbreak of war. My grandparents had sent me a postcard with their photographs, passport size, pasted to it. I used to look at it a lot once the separation had become final, the silence broken only by a rare Red Cross letter. Some things, many things, had been left too late. It was better not to talk about them too much, not then, or even half a lifetime later. To do so was to arouse feelings of guilt and recrimination, even against the dead, which could never be stilled.

3

DAYLIGHT RAIDS began on London in June 1940, when the sirens started to wail regularly for the first time since the 'phoney war' began in September 1939. They were small-scale at first, but soon increased in intensity, culminating in what was later to be known as Battle of Britain day, September 15th, when the R.A.F. brought down so many German planes that the Luftwaffe turned to night attacks. In our outlying London suburb the raids remained small-scale, but September 15th happened to be my parents' wedding anniversary. In spite of the travel restrictions, the slow, overcrowded trains, my mother planned a family reunion.

It just so happened that my father was stationed in Cirencester at the time. We had come back from Scotland after the inevitable and immediate invasion did not take place, and my father decided to join up. It was explained to us, as children, that he considered it his moral duty to help our adopted country, which had taken us in. I was impressed by his serious resolve, even though it was still far from clear to me why we had changed sides, though the general consensus of opinion, even amongst English people who had never been there, seemed to be that Germany was now full of bad people. Well, they were trying to attack England, for a start.

My respect for my father increased by leaps and bounds. His resolve to volunteer, and the serious tone in which he explained his decision, shared by my mother, put him into the ranks of heroes of legend and romance. This was a far, far better thing than he or most men had ever done, and my brother and I were proud of him, and felt honoured by the fact that he had confided in us. Yes, we agreed, we thought he ought to go, even though we would miss him. Since then we had not seen him, this father of ours who had become a soldier, and throughout the long, uncomfortable train journey excitement mounted at the prospect of seeing him in his new identity after such a long absence. We arrived in the small town, its narrow streets crowded with shoppers and men in uniform going off duty. And suddenly, coming up Cricklade Street towards the Market Place, there he was, walking to meet us in the uniform we had never seen. The excitement was too much for my six-year-old brother. He broke into a run and yelled at the top of his voice: 'Daddy! How many Germans have you killed?'

My father held out his arms and laughed. Several passers-by stopped on the narrow pavement outside Woolworth's and laughed at the little boy. I allowed myself to smile, a little embarrassed, with the superior wisdom and restraint of my eight years to his six. I had sensed that his remark was inappropriate, though I was not sure why. Possibly there were no Germans in Gloucestershire who had to be killed.

The truth, when my father began to talk, was very down-to-earth. He did not even have a gun. Since he had joined the Pioneer Corps he had done a lot of rough manual work: at the moment he was digging a trench to supply water for a new camp up the Whiteway. So far none of the foreigners had been issued with guns, only wooden sticks. He laughed at his situation, at the whole situation—a bunch of highly qualified men doing the roughest unskilled labour because they were German and Austrian refugees, and thus untrustworthy. Throughout his six years in the army he kept his spirits up by small acts of defiance against British officers which were recounted in great detail and with much satisfaction when he came home on leave.

My father did not stop being a hero. At least as far as I was concerned, he became one of a different sort for the duration of the war: a man who put up with physical discomforts and a rough life without complaint; who slept in a bunk, ate food from a tin plate, wore heavy boots and rough khaki, had no privacy, and never complained. Who got shunted around, drilled and marched about with a heavy pack on his back, soaked to the skin, covered in mud, ordered about, slept in a

Nissen hut, and always came back cheerful, as though he had returned from a ludicrous camp for boys. During his absences he wrote long letters on blue regulation paper and saved his chocolate ration for our delight.

Adapting to life in a foreign country which is fighting for survival, and where you are known as an 'enemy alien' has its drawbacks, and we all felt them in different ways. We always gave 'stateless' as our nationality, and were strictly forbidden to speak German at any time, but particularly on public transport. Towards the end of the war, when my father was already with the invading forces in France, my mother got particularly bitter about having to report at the police station each time she left the district for a short trip, but we all had a good laugh when my maiden aunt, who had dabbled in oils all her life, got arrested for painting a camouflaged airfield on one of her outdoor jaunts. She never strayed abroad without carrying at least one alarm clock in her baggage, and when one of these went off at the local police station she succeeded in causing a bomb scare.

But the population of Cirencester was not particularly xenophobic. In 1940 they had a Free Polish air force unit stationed nearby, and my father's Pioneer Corps had taken over the Bingham Hall. Other troops came, took over hotels and requisitioned buildings, and left again. There was a constant coming and going, and to add to all this upheaval the second great influx of civilian evacuees had begun as the bombing of the big cities began in earnest. These evacuees were welcomed with considerably less enthusiasm than the first lot, who came in September 1939 and gradually drifted back home during the lull of the phoney war. A woman who worked in the W.V.S. recalled how the first batch of unaccompanied children were welcomed in the Corn Hall with tears, tea and sentiment, but that enthusiasm soon wore thin with the reality of everyday problems. By 1940 many people had hastily let their spare rooms, or found relatives to occupy them, before the second wave of evacuees hit the town.

In comparison with the lower-class hordes who invaded the town and caused much consternation on account of their lack of clean underwear and Christian upbringing, foreigners who came to the area, far from being resented, acquired a certain glamour. A good deal of fraternising seems to have gone on with German prisoners of war who came to work on the land, an unimaginable situation in London where, towards the end of the war, they were occasionally to be seen digging up drains. As children we glared at them or, even more damning, pretended not to see them.

Souvenirs of friendships with P.O.W.s are kept in Cirencester homes. The many Poles who settled in the town after the war are referred to with some pride. And the memory of the Pioneer Corps in those far off days still lingers on. Educated chaps. Most of them had never done manual work before. Didn't know one end of a spade from the other. After the drain up the long stretch of the Whiteway was finished they were put in with the New Zealand Foresters, to chop down trees.

Their commanding officer never went back to New Zealand and still lives in the area, retired now, an elderly but upright gentleman. He remembers the Pioneer Corps. I told him my father was one. 'I had nothing but sympathy for your chaps,' he said kindly, but with an unmistakable trace of the old army officer in his way of speaking. 'They found timbering very tough. They were very intelligent men, who'd never done physical work before. But they learned fast, and later they were just as good as my men.' The task was to chop down some of the finest beechwood in England, in the forests of Cirencester Park, to build Mosquito planes. The whole of Hailey Wood was felled. Other wood went to the Navy. The New Zealanders spent three years on the task. At the end of the war they went back home, taking some of the local girls with them, including Jack's sister.

According to the Colonel, the Pioneer Corps also had a reputation for giving good parties, and their cooking was so good that the Pioneer Corps was held up as a model for the rest of the army, by the Catering Officer of Southern Command, for their skill at making the best of army rations. 'Not like my chaps,' added the Colonel, 'who were a pretty rough lot.' An estimation confirmed by old photographs, in the local newspaper of the period, of brawny tree-felling champions who regularly entertained the town with exhibitions of their skill on a Saturday afternoon.

For men who had known persecution, a rough outdoor life had its compensations. Physical release, the sleep of sheer weariness, and an immediate escape from brooding anxiety. The Colonel recalled a remark made by one of the Pioneers under his command, that he had never been so happy before in his life. It had obviously made an impression on him, that remark, though I doubt whether he fully understood it. How could he have appreciated how much more there was to such a remark than satisfaction at a healthy outdoor life? He could have no inkling, nobody could, at the release from years of stress and terror such a remark revealed. To know that you have to live through it.

★　　★　　★

We had only come for a short visit, but as the train rattled into the outskirts of London the dark night outside shook with constant explosions. My mother decided it had been a mistake to return. We would go back as soon as possible.

4

IT IS THIS second journey to Cirencester I remember. The weather was still very hot, the compartment packed, mostly with women and young children, and in those days trains did not run to schedule. The journey was slow, halting, with frequent stops in the middle of nowhere, with nothing to look at except an overgrown embankment. The journey was made more uncomfortable by a small boy who would not sit still, who clambered over everybody in his attempts to get out of the half-open window and put an end to himself. His mother was one of those weary working-class women, worn out by the unequal struggle, by broken nights, the slow soporific journey in the stuffy compartment, and perhaps the sheer persistent destructive energy of her child. Who knows, perhaps she would not have minded if he had gone out of the window for good. Anyhow, she made no attempt to restrain him as he clambered over me in his attempts to get out, so it was left to my mother to pick him off the window and put him back on his mother's lap.

The child had a persistent hacking cough. He coughed into my face quite hard before my mother picked him up by the armpits and handed him back to his indifferent mother. Within a few days of our being found a temporary billet in the Victorian terrace house of a friendly old lady whose entrance hall remained memorable on account of a black and white tiled floor and a door richly inlaid with stained glass, I was put to bed with whooping cough. I lay in a front room all alone for many hours, in a large old-fashioned bed, staring at the white haze of sunlight caught in the net curtains. The day was very long and strangely quiet. Occasionally my mother would appear at the door to make sure I was all right, and disappear again.

The miseries of whooping cough are unknown to post-war generations. It is a wretched, weakening complaint, and the whoops are the worst, a retching spasm which is also embarrassingly conspicuous in a quiet little street, amongst strangers. I tried to suppress my whoops as I took my first tottering steps down Victoria Road to the bridge where shallow water ran over pebbles and boulders to help form the source of Thames. This modest trickle of water continued to be the source of considerable wonderment to me throughout my childhood: I could not understand how such a small stream could possibly become the mighty and famous Thames at some mysterious spot unknown to me only a short distance away. The shallow was also the source of much local pride.

I was still coughing and retching when, a few days later, a lady in a green W.V.S. uniform arrived by car to drive us to a more permanent billet. A farm, she said, turning right across the bridge, past open fields. She turned off the road and stopped on a gravel path where a few chickens picked their way along the grass verge, beside a house of Cotswold stone with a walled garden. There were flowerbeds, and the lawn had been marked out as a tennis court. We stood on the gravel path as the W.V.S. lady rang the bell. A dog began to bark, and when a stout woman pulled back the door with one hand she was trying to restrain an excited wire-haired terrier with the other.

And then I was put back to bed, a different room in a strange house, where I could spend the long boring hours staring at the plain yellowish walls.

★   ★   ★

Once I got over the whooping cough I began to enjoy myself. I had never been on a farm before, which so far had been a concept derived from highly coloured children's books. The reality was infinitely more fascinating, and I spent my days running around, looking at things, animals, sniffing and smelling and poking my head into dark corners, watching people work as I followed them around. I was not going to school yet, so I had all day.

The house was roomy and old-fashioned, with a lot of dark wood, and a 'secret' staircase from the farmhouse kitchen on to the first-floor landing which intrigued me more than anything. No doubt it was originally merely a servants' staircase two centuries earlier, when the house served as the country retreat for the grand folk at the Abbey only half a mile away, but for me the steep dark stairs enclosed by doors at top and bottom were alive with exciting adventures involving smugglers and dissidents hiding from the King's men. The staircase was hardly used in those days, more of a glory hole than anything else, but I managed to get up and down it somehow several times a day, landing with excited triumph back in the farmhouse kitchen, where the farmer's wife watched me with tolerant amusement as she worked at the huge oak table.

She was always hard at work, preparing a chicken or kneading dough in the kitchen with its window seat overlooking the enclosed, flagstoned courtyard outside the back door. It was dark, cool and roomy with its stone floor and dark oak dresser, doors and shutters. Sometimes I would follow her across the small flagstoned courtyard to the buttery, and watch with amazement how she made the churn turn with her strong arms, putting enormous energy into it, as though her life depended on it. I had never seen a woman do something so vehemently forceful before. And I would accompany her to the edge of the field beyond the outhouses where the henhouses stood. The prepared chicken feed provided a distraction, but there was a wild squawking and a frantic fluttering of feathers as the hens were disturbed and the day's eggs collected in a bucket.

The menfolk were friendly but more remote. They disappeared for long hours and when they did turn up near the house they were often preoccupied. They took their work seriously, handling heavy machinery, bringing the cows back for milking. The farmer, seeing us hanging around, set us to work: we collected acorns to feed to the pigs, grubbing around under the trees in the long grass verge by the footpath.

The men were also in charge of death. It was they who struggled to catch pigs in their sties: from the high piercing squeals it was obvious that, once taken away in the lorry, they would be killed for bacon. The pigs knew it, so I was in no doubt. And one morning I watched a man catch a hen which had been wandering on the grass verge by the house and wring its neck. I was horrified by what I saw. When I came back indoors the dead chicken was hanging upside down by its claws in the courtyard. Ready for plucking and the oven. So that was how it worked.

We had a room at the side of the house, overlooking the large cowsheds, by far the most modern part of the farmstead. They looked rather like aeroplane hangars, enough so for the nearby orchard to be pitted with bomb craters. From the start I sensed that my mother did not get on as well with the farmer's wife as I would have wished her to do. She did not seem as enraptured of the sights and sounds of the farm as I was. I put it down to nerves and bought an egg for a halfpenny from the farmer's wife, which I beat up raw in a glass with pepper and salt. I had been told this was an infallible pick-me-up, and I mixed it up secretly (with my back turned at the other end of the room) and made her swallow it. She smiled kindly, with the expression of an invalid who knows such treatment to be useless, however touching the gesture, and swallowed it. There was no magical transformation, which I found rather disappointing. Ever since eggs had been in short supply my mother had been in the habit of speaking of the quite magical properties of such things as prairie oysters. Later on in the war, as we chewed our way wearily through fish and chips for the third time in a week, she would wax lyrical about the exquisite flavour and texture of an egg dish known as an omelette. I looked forward to my first omelette as one of the delights that lay waiting beyond the moon, in that inconceivable millennium known as 'after the war', and it turned out to be one of the great disappointments of my life. I discovered that omelettes, far from being an exquisite delicacy, were leathery, tasteless and ordinary, and I did not like them at all.

When we were not out walking my mother continued to be rather subdued and withdrawn, spending the time upstairs in our room. At night we all sat round the wooden table in the centre of the room and my mother lit the oil lamp. The farmer's wife had shown her how it functioned. It drew us all together, like moths round a flame, watching the glow rise up the glass funnel and cast weird shadows round the corners of the room. The light was enough to read by, sitting at the table, but once it had been turned out, once my mother had tucked us up for the night and withdrawn through the connecting door to the narrow room where she slept, the darkness was irrevocable.

We listened to the news at regular intervals on an old battery radio, and my small brother began to leap around with whoops of triumph when the death of Mr. Chamberlain was announced. He had somehow got it into his small head that Neville Chamberlain was a baddie, and belonged with Goebbels, Goering and that lot. After all, he was in a song, and all the Nazi leaders had songs about them. Perhaps also, he had picked up enough adult comments of a derogatory nature to make him suppose that Chamberlain was on the German side. Anyhow, he started letting out vociferous cheers whilst my mother anxiously tried to hush him up, and seemed very afraid that the rest of the household would hear him. The incident served to intensify my sense that all was not well between my mother and the rest of the household.

Was the tension between you and Mrs. S., the farmer's wife, political, I asked my mother many years later? Not at all, she answered. Two women could not get on together in the same kitchen, a problem that the evacuation authorities were very well aware of, so that the obligation to provide cooking facilities was never made compulsory. 'She was always criticising the way I did things. We don't do it that way in England, she'd say.'

The farmer's wife, with her strong stout body and the arms that kneaded and churned, baked and plucked, chopped and floured, reigned supreme in that cool old farmhouse kitchen with the heavy oak table and the stone floor. I was allowed to play in there, cadge titbits, run up and down the 'secret' staircase, but my mother hardly ever ventured down there, and when she did so it was very much on sufferance. We took to lunching out in the town, and became regulars in a small first-floor restaurant just behind the Market Place where the menu was as predictable as the dark wood furnishings. 'Rice pudding and stewed pears,' the waitress used to chant, as though she had never seen us before, 'or apple tart and custard.' The puddings were always the same, and we began to find it a bit of a giggle. The climax came one memorable day when she began:

'Rice pudding and stewed pears, or apple tart——'

'—And custard,' my brother chipped in wearily.

'No,' she said coldly, in her starchiest manner, 'there isn't any custard today.'

We looked sheepish, stunned into silence. Something had happened. Today was different. There was a war on. Today there was no custard.

* * *

Being an evacuee involved a lot of walking. It was a way of passing the time. My brother and I had still not been enrolled in a school, and for mothers who had come to a safe area with their children it was an escape from a house which did not belong to them, and where they had no domestic function. Going for long walks was one way of not stretching the tolerance of the householder too far.

And since one was in a town where we had no acquaintances, we walked and came back, walked and came back, simply to tire ourselves out. But sometimes we would go down to the Bingham Hall, and linger outside the heavy stone building in the hopes of catching a glimpse of my father. If a soldier saw us hanging around he would ask his name and go off to try and find him. Smiles, a few self-conscious words, and he was gone again, to polish boots or 'kitchen fatigue', which, he explained, meant peeling vast quantities of potatoes. Sometimes I would catch a glimpse, through an open door, of the long rows of wooden bunks where the men had to sleep.

The path alongside the farmhouse and walled orchard led, at right angles, to an avenue of delicately leafed trees, a wooded footpath which ended at the iron gate on Grove Lane, opposite the surviving Saxon gateway to the Abbey grounds. Usually we had this path to ourselves, quiet, smelling intimately of damp earth, but one day an elderly woman walking a pekinese dog came towards us from the gate. Perhaps nothing would have occurred if we had not been followed by the farmhouse sheep-dog. A wild dogfight ensued, with much yapping from the lapdog and not much more than high-spirited fun from the working dog. My mother tried to catch the sheepdog by the collar, whilst the lady began to call my mother a lot of rather rude names, whilst she struggled to rescue her pet. To our childish glee she fell headlong in the mud whilst trying to capture her yapping pet. My mother, who had by this time caught the sheepdog and was using the belt of her dress as a leash, apologised in halting tones. We did not know the dog had followed us, it belonged to the farm. The lady, who had heard my mother's voice and called her a bloody foreigner, or words to the usual effect, told her she had no right to be walking along this path, that she was trespassing. My mother murmured apologies and we slunk back the way we had come, dog in tow. But for us children nothing could spoil the glory of that moment when the bad-tempered lady had fallen headlong in the mud. It was as good as a funny film.

The next morning there was a ring at the front door of the farmhouse, a fairly unusual occurrence in itself, since most people used the back door. On the doorstep stood the owner of the pekinese, and she asked to speak to my mother. She said she was sorry for the way she had spoken to her, as a good Christian she had not been able to sleep the previous night, and would my mother join her knitting circle.

This incident caused a sensation, and the anecdote of the day Mrs. D. came to apologise was handed down in the farmer's family from generation to generation. The farmer's wife told her daughter-in-law about it when Jack got married after the war, and the story was remembered when I went back to the farmhouse a lifetime later, though the three of us had been forgotten. Because Mrs. D. was 'county'. She and her husband lived in the large mansion on the other side of Grove Lane, and in those days the county families ruled over the town by virtue of who they were. The fact that she had been extremely rude, the added fact that we were not trespassing anyhow, was somehow irrelevant: but Mrs. D. had come to apologise. To local folk it was as though Zeus had come down from Olympus.

It was the autumn of 1940, England's darkest hour, but on the Bathurst estate his lordship's hounds were being groomed for another foxhunting season, and Major and Mrs. D, who were tenants of the Abbey, the second great house of the area, still kept a staff of twelve and somehow avoided having any evacuees foisted on them, although the house was extremely large, even allowing for twelve servants.

Not that the county did not do their bit when war came. They had been deciding what was good for the town for centuries, and the outbreak of war gave them an excellent opportunity to exercise their skills of leadership. Lord Bathurst, whose ancestors had built the local museum, the cattle market, and given the go-ahead for the first railway line (not forgetting to buy some shares as well), now reviewed the Home Guard and opened a mobile canteen raised by public subscription for troops stationed in the town. Their ladies, meanwhile, were busy sitting on committees concerned with the welfare of evacuee children, even if they did decline to take them into their own homes. And they ran knitting circles. Everybody not actually in uniform was hard at work, knitting for victory.

On two afternoons a week my mother would walk over to the Abbey, so-called because it stood in the grounds of the Augustine abbey which had controlled the town until the dissolution of the monasteries during the reign of Henry VIII. His daughter Elizabeth had made over the Abbey estates to her physician, Richard Master, and his descendants own the land to this day. At the house my mother's continental style of knitting caused a mild sensation, because it involves holding the thread across the left forefinger and merely giving a quick twitch for each stitch, instead of laboriously bringing the wool forward and back with the right hand, English fashion. The local women tried to copy her, but it is hard to relearn the skills of a lifetime overnight. There is no doubt about it, had the outcome of the war depended primarily on the nation's knitting effort, Germany would certainly have won. In fact my mother's knitting speed was relatively slow: once she had taught me the rudiments I was soon much faster than her, and before the war was finally won I was able to contribute any number of scarves, gloves, and balaclava helmets to the war effort.

Lilias, Lady Bathurst also ran a knitting circle at Cirencester House, where her husband's ancestor had once entertained Pope to the more sophisticated pleasures of wining, dining, and gambling at cards. No doubt there must have been a competitive element between the various knitting groups run by such ladies. Certainly Lady Bathurst lost no opportunity to publicise her group's achievements by writing to the local paper at regular intervals, and of course the *Wiltshire and Gloucestershire Standard* respectfully published her letters. In October 1940 she reported that her knitting circle had now made 2,000 garments, knitted and otherwise, including pyjamas, bed-jackets, pullovers and seaboot socks. Presumably the bed-jackets were intended for the Memorial Hospital—also an object of her charity and founded by a Bathurst in memory of his first wife—rather than for the gallant boys in blue or khaki.

Other, more humble groups were also busy doing their bit to help the war effort. At the Council School boys of seven and upward were industriously knitting during their playtime. The headmaster told a local reporter that knitting had replaced bookbinding to help the war effort, and one seven-year-old had 'already completed two full-length scarves, a balaclava helmet, and a hot-water bottle cover'. One does rather wonder where the last item ended up. The Picture House, the older of the town's two cinemas, had become a collecting depot for woollens made for the Navy: the manager had announced a scheme which embraced three classes of lady—those who could knit and afford to purchase their own wool, those who could knit but could not afford to buy the wool, and those who could not knit but could afford to buy the wool and pass it on to those who could. Probably as good a way as any of defining the three classes of society without being divisive in a time of national emergency.

Although I was to become a skilled and rapid knitter I was just beginning in the autumn of 1940. My mother took me into the wool shop in Cricklade Street and bought me enough khaki hanks to make my uncle, also stationed in the town as a soldier in the Pioneer Corps, a scarf for his birthday. Made entirely in garter stitch, which was all I knew, it grew increasingly odd: the edges seemed to wander about in an uneven fashion, and one or two stitches got lost and could not be found again, however assiduously I poked about in the khaki mesh. Eventually my mother helped me to cast off. My uncle kissed me on the cheek and said it was beautiful. I was intelligent enough to suspect him of lying, though in the nicest possible way.

*　　*　　*

The Abbey had extensive grounds, which were occasionally opened to the public during the war for functions planned to raise funds for the war effort. The huge eighteenth-century mansion stood on the site of the original Elizabethan house, which had been partly constructed from masonry left strewn about when Henry VIII ordered the Augustine abbey to be pulled down.

Mrs. D. ran a knitting circle, whilst her husband the Major kindly opened the grounds, which included part of the Roman fortifications, for such functions as tree-felling exhibitions given by the New Zealand Foresters. Although Mrs D. did not have any evacuees, the billeting officer of those days recollected that the Major had been good enough to house Scottish steel erectors over the stables. The billeting officer explained that Scottish steel erectors were a pretty rough lot, and not everyone would have liked them over their stables.

But then few people had stables. Reports of meetings of the Cirencester Rural District Council in 1940 and 1941 reflect a growing tussle between householders, the Council, and the Ministry. In August 1940 'the Ministry had been informed that the district had reached saturation point as regards accommodation' but the Ministry had intimated that a further two hundred children would be sent to the area if it became necessary. One member of the Council, Colonel Elwes, proposed that they should object to more evacuee children being sent to the area, since it would mean too great a strain on the local services, such as sewerage and water. He foresaw a serious epidemic if more children were sent.

The same issue of the newspaper advertised 'Pleasant and comfortable place for Housemaid; 2 in family; 3 maids.' And a few months later Mrs. D. at the Abbey advertised: 'Kitchen-maid wanted with experience; good references; 3 in kitchen; staff 12; 3 in dining-room.' Meanwhile, less privileged house-holders and landlords were informed that they were now subject to the Rent Restrictions Act, owing to the exceptional demand for accommodation, and that exorbitant demands for rent would result in a fine of not less than £100.

At local level, far from Fleet Street and Whitehall, the restrictions of wartime censorship had to be interpreted on the spot. Awkward, and possibly open to abuse. Although the deliberations of the Rural District Council were reported in considerable detail, local grumbles to the effect that the allocation of evacuees was not being conducted fairly, and that some very large houses had got off scot free, were, curiously enough, considered sufficiently useful to the enemy to be suppressed by the editor. A columnist, grumbling about wartime censorship, hinted at the problem and gave away enough information to record that a sense of injustice did exist locally.

By November 1940 a meeting of the Cirencester Urban District Council had decided that it was now necessary to exercise compulsory powers in billeting evacuees. The Council came to this conclusion reluctantly, but had no alternative on account of the pressure being brought by the Ministry of Health in relation to the reception of more evacuees. 'Mr. Winstone said it was understood that the Billeting Officer had been having a rather rough time at the hands of some householders, and he (Mr. Winstone) thought it should be made clear to the public that the Billeting Officer had the backing of that Council in the exercise of his duties. (Hear, hear.)' A subsequent report of the W.V.S., who handled the day-to-day problems of finding accommodation for evacuees, revealed that, although the increasing influx since September 1940 had made it necessary to resort to compulsory billeting, 'in every case the threat of compulsion had induced the householder to agree voluntarily'. A staff of thirty W.V.S. welfare officers kept in constant touch with the evacuees to solve the inevitable difficulties.

However, by 1941 hostility to the invasion of evacuees had obviously reached a new fever pitch, at least in some bosoms. The local newspaper published an article by a certain Dr. Bryn Thomas, suggesting that any further evacuees should be housed in specially constructed huts 'near a water supply and a shop'. Dr. Thomas suggested that each hut should house 100 men or women, sleeping in hammocks which could be stowed away during the day. In this way, he added, the 'initiative of the evacuees would be utilised to the best purpose, a factor of no small importance.' The notion sounds like a British style concentration camp, infused with the Boy Scout spirit of Baden-Powell. The character-building virtues of self-help are regularly preached by those who do not want to give help to those in desperate need. Fortunately the plan did not meet with Ministry approval.

*   *   *

Times have changed since 1941, when Mrs. D. advertised for an extra kitchenmaid to add to her staff of twelve. In those days no one had the temerity to suggest that the vast suites of rooms could have given shelter to a few evacuees, let alone invoke the threat of compulsory powers. Probably it never occurred to those in charge of finding rooms and more rooms for the bedraggled and weary stream of people who arrived each day at the railway station, that it was feasible to ask such grand county folk to change their way of life. But after the war was over it became increasingly hard to find tenants for such a vast mansion, and it was finally pulled down in 1965. There is a small housing estate, but most of the grounds have become a public park. Now anyone may walk across the wide lawns, sit by the water, stare at the Roman remains of Corinium's outer wall, or walk through the old Abbey gatehouse.

5

As a child I only saw the Abbey grounds from the outside: a long stone wall which ran the length of Grove Lane as far as the London Road and down the lane from the crossroads into the town. Beyond the wall were high trees enclosing a silence which might have been death. It was only after I had been marching in crocodile for some months that it occurred to me to enquire what lay behind the high grey wall that went on and on: that it first struck my consciousness as an oddity of territorial exclusivity which shut me, and people like me, out. I could not look over the top, or see through the dense trees. If you have to walk in crocodile it is no fun to skirt a long grey wall. The little house above the heavy wooden gates studded with iron looked old, but the gates were always firmly closed. I did not know that the gateway was the oldest structure in the entire town, and had been used by the monks of the first religious foundation, before the Normans came.

When the Normans arrived the town became a royal manor, much favoured for hunting, but was soon given over to the foundation of an Augustine abbey. For centuries the Abbot was a despotic overlord, exploiting the rights he had been given and taking over some he had not. When the angry citizens took their grievances to Westminster they found that the Abbot had not only God but the King, whom he had bribed, on his side.

After Henry VIII had the monastery pulled down in 1539 the town was taken over by the new nobility, the new landed gentry who had done well in trade or found favour at Court. The Masters came first, with their personal links with Queen Elizabeth, and took over the Abbey lands for the sum of £590. A century later the Bathursts arrived. In 1695 Sir Benjamin

Bathurst, a governor of the African and also of the East India Company, bought the manor of Little Oakley to the west of the town, together with its Elizabethan manor house. The family, helped by useful connections with Queen Anne, prospered, bought several adjacent estates until they became the biggest landowners in the area, and were duly ennobled by Queen Anne for political services rendered. Or rather, a Bathurst was created Baron with eleven other peers to strengthen her Tory ministry, and the earldom came half a century later.

Freed from the religious yoke of the Abbot, the citizens of Cirencester now found themselves hemmed in by two powerful landowners: the Masters to the north of the town, and the Bathursts to the west. Needless to say these two families also elected themselves as spokesmen for the good people of the town. For centuries, by a gentleman's agreement, each family controlled one of the two seats to the House of Commons, and the two Members, duly elected or returned unopposed, were invariably called Bathurst or Master, unless the families ran out of a suitable son for a short period and selected a nominee. This amicable arrangement worked smoothly for several centuries, to the detriment of no one but the people of Cirencester, except on one occasion, when, in 1754, Lord Bathurst broke the agreement and nominated two of his sons instead of only one. This unfortunate breach of faith resulted in an election riot, a pitched battle between two mobs, and the death of a Bathurst supporter, an ordinary, no doubt ignorant, unpoliticised man whose name was Jordan.

But soon a third family was to throw its gauntlet into the political arena. The Cripps family, unlike the landed gentry established in a previous age, were representative of a prosperous new middle class. They owned no land, but had grown rich through banking and brewery businesses in the town. Throughout the nineteenth century they were often in possession of one of the Parliamentary seats, while their interest in local government extended well into the twentieth century. Joseph Cripps M.P. was Chairman of the Board of Guardians from its inception in 1837. In May 1926 a Major Cripps retired from the chairmanship of the Board after twenty-six years on the Board of Guardians, half of that time as Chairman.

The General Strike was going on at the time, but that had little effect on the town, apart from interrupting train services. The *Wiltshire and Gloucestershire Standard*, which had begun as a high Tory, rabidly anti-reform newspaper in 1837, and gradually calmed down over the years as the prospects of anarchy and revolution faded, was published as usual from its offices in Dyer Street, and could report that life in Cirencester had remained unaffected by the Strike, apart from the fact that one or two workers, who belonged to a union, did not report for work.

Almost untouched by the effects of the industrial revolution, life changed very slowly in Cirencester. Increasingly dependent on patronage and benevolent paternalism, the local townsfolk, tradesmen and tenant farmers had acquired an attitude of awe and servility to the local gentry, particularly anyone called Bathurst, Chester-Master (the Masters obtained a double-barrel at the beginning of this century) or Cripps. Even the introduction of the secret ballot in the 1870s, which the *Standard* had once condemned as 'unmanly and un-English', did not entirely finish Cirencester as a pocket borough, though it had lost one seat. Elderly inhabitants alive today can recall Benjamin Bathurst, who held the seat with only one interruption for twenty years and retired in 1918, when Cirencester and Tewkesbury were amalgamated. Local irreverent legend has it that the only words he ever spoke during those years in the House of Commons were: 'Could someone open a window?'

It was about time someone did.

*   *   *

An outsider who came to live in Cirencester in the years just before the war, for many years the local librarian, was struck by the relationship between the local gentry and ordinary towns-folk. Before the war, he told me, ladies would drive into the Market Place and wait for shopkeepers to come out in the rain to take their orders.

War may have given the small town new priorities, but old

attitudes did not fade away overnight. Mrs. D. was used to being able to bark orders at people—'She could be a bit of an old dragon', Jack remembered. She was also used to walking alone and undisturbed on land which did not belong to her, though it formed part of the same old estate, and it took her a night's reflection to realise that the town was now crammed with strangers who did not know the customs of the area or, for that matter, recognise her for who she was. When she came round to the farmhouse to apologise, it was because my mother was a stranger to the district, and ignorant of the fact that she should not have been walking down that tree-lined path. My mother was left with the impression that she had been trespassing, when she had been doing nothing of the sort, and was duly impressed by the big-hearted generosity of her gesture in coming round to clarify the misunderstanding.

We avoided the pleasant avenue after that, though sometimes, on our own, my brother and I would sneak down it with our hearts in our mouths, in terror of meeting the angry lady with her yapping dog. We never did. It was always deserted, slightly melancholy, with the mists of winter closing in, a few last gold leaves on the high denuded trees, dead leaves trodden into the earth smelling of damp and decay, and the creaking iron gate at the far end.

It has gone now, the last vestige of the old estate, connecting the farmhouse to the Abbey. There is a new housing estate where the long grey wall once stood, and the iron gate was removed when the lane was widened into a dual carriageway as a town by-pass. The trees that remain are wired off to discourage walkers, since part of the land is now used for public sports facilities. But the wire is unnecessary: what remains of the old avenue is choked in a tangle of thick undergrowth, whilst the branches of the untended trees meet in a wilderness as dark as the entrance to a dream.

The tone of hauteur common to the local gentry is evident in the reports of blackout offences heard at Cirencester Petty Sessions. There was a spate of such proceedings throughout the country in the first year of the war, and assiduous local constables seem to have had less than the expected reverence for their betters when it came to rendering assistance to the Germans by showing a light. So whilst ordinary mortals apologised to the bench, could not for the life of them imagine how the offence had occurred in the first place, promised not to do it again and paid their fines without demur, the gentry were often less humble. 'Lights will not stop the war, and you can caution me as much as you like,' one titled lady told a visiting constable, whilst a major charged with showing a light told the presiding magistrate: 'This house was let to me some weeks ago by a local firm of estate agents and they have not provided me with blackout materials; until they do I will not be responsible for the blackout.' As the major had been warned on two previous occasions, he obviously meant what he said, but the chairman of the bench said it was a bad case and fined him.

Not that they were unpatriotic. Far from it. Most of them were only too anxious to help, but it had to be on their own terms. The billeting officer had been very understanding when Lilias Bathurst refused to have evacuees in the vast mansion which is Cirencester House, and did not try to use the threat of a compulsory order. He did, however, exert a certain amount of pressure to get her to accept soldiers in the rooms above her stables, which she was also reluctant to do. But when the local Women's Institute organised a lecture on fruit bottling she took the trouble to sit down and write one of her not infrequent letters to the *Standard:* 'During the last war my housekeeper, Mrs. Pearson, taught the Cirencester W.I. to make jam and this house became a small jam factory. I hope her method of sealing the jam has not been forgotten, but in case it has I will describe it again. . . .'

* * *

Servility has not always been the overriding tone of the towns-people of Cirencester towards the gentry who controlled their lives, and occasionally men have died for a less absurd cause than the claim of Earl Bathurst's sons to represent the people of Cirencester by virtue of his power of eviction as the biggest landlord in the district. In 1312 Master Nicholas of Stratton impleaded Abbot Adam in the Exchequer for levying tallage for his own purposes. The suit went on for nine years, during which time the abbot quietly procured pardons for the encroachments alleged against him, and won his case. Nicholas of Stratton was cudgelled to death by the abbot's men.

But a more momentous death is commemorated in a modest brass plate on the west wall of the parish church:

HERE LYETH BYRIED THE BODY OF
HODKINSON PAINE, CLOTHIER,
WHO DIED THE 3rd of FEB 1642

The poore's supplie his life & calling grac't,
    till warres made rents & PAINE from poor displac't.
But what made poore unfortunate PAINE blest,
    by warre they lost their PAINE, yet found no rest
Hee looseing quiet, by warre yet gained ease
    by it PAINES life began and paines did cease,
And from the troubles here him God did sever
    by death to life, by warre to peace for ever.

During the Civil War the attitude of the local gentry was ambivalent, but the townspeople were fiercely anti-royalist. When Lord Chandos, the Deputy Lieutenant, arrived in the town for a meeting with the county gentry to put up at the Ram Inn, his coach was hacked to pieces by the infuriated inhabitants, and he only managed to escape with the help of the Master family and the Pooles, at that time the incumbents of the other manor house. The townspeople had already repelled Prince Rupert's troops once, but he came back with reinforcements and took the town by assault from the west, at Cecily Hill and the watermill near Barton House, where Hodkinson Paine was killed with the colours in his hand.

It was a humiliating defeat. The preparations had been extensive, and the streets had been barricaded with chains, harrows and wagons, with an iron six pounder in the Market Place and fortifying walls and more guns at strategic points of the outskirts of the town, including a brass cannon in Sir William Master's garden, the Abbey grounds. But it was not enough. The local commander had weakened the town's defences by sending troops to assist in the battle for Sudeley Castle. John White, in his description of the fall of Cirencester, spoke proudly of 'a very hot fight for some two hours' at Barton, 'during all which time, we lost but one man . . . who could not find his way forth through the fire and smoke', but wrote with bitterness about 'the treachery of our malignant gentry round about us, who constantly gave the enemy intelligence, and entertainment in their house, made provision for their armies, and some of them appeared in armes before their neighbour towne, which they could endure to see both fired and spoyled'.

No doubt John White was right in his assessment. Sir Henry Poole, whose estate was on the west side of the town, from where the successful assault had come, was married to a sister of Lord Chandos and was wholly on the King's side. Sir William Master's attitude seems to have vacillated according to who was winning at the time, and he entertained King Charles to supper and a bed for the night while the town remained in Royalist hands.

Over a thousand of the local townspeople were taken prisoner, stripped, and imprisoned in the church overnight, 'and though many of them were wounded and weary, yet their friends were not suffered to bring them a cup of water into the church that night, but what they thrust in at the backside of the church, having broken the windowes'. The prisoners were bound and marched off to Oxford, to make their abject submission to the King, whilst his troops stripped the town of cloth, wool and yarn, and the surrounding countryside of livestock.

On the night of September 15th 1643, a Parliamentary army, 15,000 strong, which had marched from London under the command of Essex, took sleeping Cirencester by surprise, captured the entire royalist garrison and their provisions, and marched on, abandoning the small town, which was then used as a base for royalist manoeuvres.

Twenty years later, in 1663, Charles II and his Queen were entertained at Cirencester House as the guests of Lord Newburgh, whose wife was the daughter of Sir Henry Poole. The wool industry had been in decline during the reign of his father and grandfather, but business improved in the town when, in 1679, Charles II made it compulsory for the dead to be buried in wool, thus giving a boost to the industry. When Defoe visited Cirencester in around 1700 he found it 'still a very good town, populous and rich, full of clothiers, and driving a great trade in wool'.

In the West Country the clothier controlled the wool industry, buying raw material and selling finished cloth after it had been sent out to the various craftsmen, an entrepreneur who relied heavily on the poorest workers of all, the women spinning in their cottages in outlying villages and hamlets. Defoe commented that many of these clothiers 'now pass for gentry' and were worth between ten and forty thousand pounds. After the bourgeois revolution for which Hodkinson Paine had died holding the flag, they could align themselves with their old enemies, the gentry, and live in almost as much comfort and style. They were not interested in investing their money in new-fangled machinery, when weavers, in their own workshops, would work a fourteen-hour day, and seventeen hours in summer, when daylight lasted longer. When spinning schools were started as a form of poor relief, and Cirencester boasted a school endowed for the purpose of teaching poor children frame-knitting, founded under the will of Mrs. Rebecca Powell in 1722. Labour was cheap, and as beneficiaries of Britain's premier industry for centuries, they no doubt slept easy in their country mansions, secure in the knowledge that, as Defoe wrote in 1724: 'Be their country hot or cold, torrid or frigid, 'tis the same thing, near the Equinox or near the Pole, the English woollen manufacturer clothes them all.'

But times were changing. New machinery was invented, cotton arrived. By the beginning of the nineteenth century the woollen industry in Cirencester was dead. 'There is at present only one clothing-house in this town,' wrote the local historian Samuel Rudder in 1800, 'which employs the same stock-mill that Leland mentions to have been built by John Blake, the last abbot of Cirencester, besides another seven or eight miles distant.' The abbot's mill had been new in 1539. Cirencester was not unique in failing to keep up with the times. The whole of the Gloucestershire woollen industry lost its lead with the industrial revolution. By 1834 Lancashire had 1,142 power

44

looms for wool, and Gloucestershire had a mere four. Many people would say that the sleepy, picturesque town had a lucky escape. Other small industries took over, and there was enough work for a small town which stayed small.

6

As CHILDREN we thought it was a cathedral, with its vast porch opening on to the Market Place, its even bigger nave, the stonework fluted and pinnacled, and highest of all, the great tower. Afterwards I thought that the church would shrink just as the narrow lanes of small houses had done, that in our awe of the gothic structure we had been deluded by the disproportions of childhood. But when I saw it again the shining white edifice was as large and impressive as ever. It had lost nothing in the interim, though it was of course a parish church and not a cathedral. One of the largest and grandest parish churches in England, a monument to civic pride over centuries, to the superb craftsmanship of local stonemasons, evidence of continuing prosperity through the ages, an ambitious piety which may have been instigated by the monastery but survived its dissolution. Early in the fifteenth century they built a high white tower which still dominates the countryside and was in its day a triumph of craftsman's will against the pull of the earth and a claim on the rewards of heaven in a sky that was dizzy and aloof; in the following century they had enough confidence and optimism to rebuild and broaden the entire nave; in the nineteenth century there was enough money available in the district for expensive restoration. The high-backed pews and galleries were removed, the flooring was taken up and some bodies, which had been interred just under the surface, were re-interred, and the floor covered with rather dull red tiles after it had been surfaced with six inches of concrete to seal in the stench of old corpses. The foundations were made secure, the battlements renewed, and the tower received a new clock with chiming apparatus. Built to take two thousand or thereabouts in the days of compulsory worship, the services are now attended by a handful of people. The latest, twentieth-century improvement is a system of loudspeakers which fills the hollow stone spaces with a distorted crackle and makes a mockery of the superb acoustics of arched stone.

The voice of the vicar lacks confidence as he grapples with the poltergeist thuds and hisses of the new microphone in an attempt to enter into the spirit of the twentieth century, but the dead have a proud assurance which nothing, and no one, can displace, and easily outnumber the living. Perhaps the bones of Hodkinson Paine were disturbed during the nineteenth-century renovations which made the church sufficiently hygienic and comfortable for the respectable classes who gathered here on a Sunday in the prosperous middle years of the last century, but if he had seen his companions in death he might have felt that the battle at Cecily Hill had not been fought in vain. Of course there are chapels and elaborate monuments to members of the Bathurst and Master families, but the marble memorials to the prosperous deceased, clothiers and other merchants, have taken their place beside them on the walls. The inscriptions betray their new wealth and sense of social position, the newly found self-esteem of respectable families who had become almost as good as the gentry. One detects a touch of smugness.

Conjugal affection has consecrated this Marble to the Memory of RICHARD SELFE ESQ^r.
Whose unaffected piety
Uniform benevolence
And inflexible integrity
Conciliated the respect and esteem of all who were connected with him
As relatives friends and neighbours
He was born Jany. 15. 1749 He died Jany. 14th 1817.

The inscriptions are also monuments to the virtues of family life:
Near this place was interred
the body of Mr JAMES CLUTTERBUCK
who died June 30th 1722, aged 49.
He left to the care of his wife Susannah Clutterbuck

a numerous family
which she brought up with parental tenderness
evincing her affection for her husband,
by a constant attention to the trust reposed in her
till she departed this life.

The tablet also records the names, ages and death dates of her children, including those who died in infancy and finishes: 'Elizabeth their youngest daughter having been first married to MR. SOMERSET DRAPER of LONDON and after his death to MR. JOHN CRIPPS and inhabitant of this town, died February 29th 1784.'

The tablets are like miniature family histories of people who felt themselves worthy of one but would otherwise go unrecorded. Even a modest literary recognition could not be taken for granted. His surviving children put up a tablet to Samuel Rudder Printer. 'His History of Gloucestershire will Establish his Character as a Writer'. His wife, 'a tender mother of EIGHT children' is mentioned, and the children who died are listed.

* * *

The great white tower of the parish church provides a landmark for miles around. It is almost always visible above the low roofs of the narrow winding streets, and if not, it will appear suddenly and unexpectedly as you come round a bend to find yourself close to the Market Place once more. No stranger could get lost in the town. No newcomer could get lost for miles around, because the square tower with its four pinnacles remains visible; from whichever road you come the tower rears up above a haze of trees though the rest of the town is drowned in the hollow. The stonework gleams white, turning to pale gold in the slanting rays of the setting sun.

The eighteenth-century splendour of Cirencester Park, planned and planted by the first Earl Bathurst, is diminished by the craftsman's tower, the people's tower, built two hundred years before his lordship took over roads, manors and acreage on an unheard-of scale to create a vast park of unprecedented proportions, with the Broad Ride leading from town to horizon and over the other side straight as a ruler for mile after wooded mile, an assertion of ownership, of man's reasonable triumph over nature and its higgledy-piggledy untidyness, its quirks and messes and sudden surprises. There is no room here for the little man, with his patch of ground and his pig in the back yard. Everything is on a grand scale: the huge house, the enormous yew hedge beyond the elaborate stone portals which always remain closed, and above all the Broad Ride. Conceived on a grand scale, it has come after two hundred years to triumphant fruition: the trees planted on either side of the grass verge are all that an avenue of trees should be, broad-branching, leafy and thick-stemmed, huge and full of *gravitas*, the dignity of age.

But it is all mocked by the tower. No matter how far you walk up the Broad Ride, if you pause for a moment to get your breath back, and turn to look townward to the ornamental iron gates and the Armoury beyond, built in the last century to look like a medieval fortress beside the genteel eighteenth-century houses of Cecily Hill, the most noticeable feature, central to the view, is the tower of the parish church. It does not seem to grow smaller as you walk further on. It dwarfs the giant beech trees. Shining white against the skyline, it seems to grow larger and more dominant, instead of receding into the distance. Whatever his lordship's intentions, the fact is: the great avenue only serves to do homage to the tower.

Pope, who had spent a good deal of time at Cirencester House, where the genial earl had allowed him to indulge his passion for planning and planting, saw the problem clearly enough. Perhaps he might have been more discreet if he had not been piqued, on visiting the estate during Bathurst's absence, to discover that the latter had carried out certain improvements and alterations without first consulting him. So he wrote to his lordship: 'As to the church steeple I am truly sorry for it, yet I would not however pull down the house. I would rather the reformation began, as reformations always ought, at the church itself. Not that I would wish the body of it entirely taken away, but only the steeple lowered. This would bring matters to some uniformity, and the dissenters and quakers would be greatly obliged as it is the high tower itself above all they hold in abomination, whereby your lordship's interest in the next elections might be vastly strengthened.'

Mockery and self-mockery in this barbed missive. Lord Bathurst was known to be friendly with the Dissenters, who had gained a strong foothold in the town. At the same time Pope, the dreamer of gardens more fantastic and splendid than anything found in mere nature, acknowledged himself defeated. That later, a local historian should have taken his suggestion to lower the steeple as serious, only completes the joke.

*   *   *

Besides the ancient parish church in the Market Place the Watermoor, developed in the last century as a Victorian housing estate, has its own church of spired Victorian gothic. The Baptists came early, and established themselves in one of the older lanes of Cotswold stone. So did the Quakers and the Unitarians, whilst the Methodists and Roman Catholics came later and built near the railway station, in dismal redbrick railway style. A small town, it has catered for every shade of Christian opinion, and in 1940 Christian opinion was still very strong. Even now the fabric of an old-fashioned Sunday still holds good, though fewer people actually bother to go to church. But the churches are there, and if people stay at home to cook a traditional family dinner they are conscious of having missed the customary observances.

In 1940 the local inhabitants were shocked to find themselves invaded by an influx of evacuees who were, in many cases, not only primitive and dirty, but also heathens. Daisy Bracher, who ran the evacuee sick bay above a shop in Cricklade Street, said prayers every night from the landing, with the doors to the various rooms ajar, so that all the children could hear her voice. She was appalled to discover that most of her charges did not have the faintest notion who Jesus was, and her shocked confrontation with the realities of city life was obviously shared by many other people in the town. For years the town had been peaceful and rather sleepy, contented and prosperous, and nothing had happened to shake it out of its deeply engrained conservatism. Even the war, when it came, had been rather remote, and the town would be spared its harsher realities. As for voluntary work, running canteens, collecting money for the Red Cross or secondhand clothes for evacuees, this was all part of a long tradition of Christian duty. Probably many people wished the war could somehow have been avoided, but now it had come they were prepared to do their bit for King and country.

But they were not prepared for some of the discoveries they made about their own country. In March 1940 the *Standard* published an article on the serious deficiencies of the English educational system as brought to light by the war. 'Among the incidental results of the evacuation scheme has been the discovery that large numbers of town children are being brought up with no religious knowledge at all.' This, wrote the author, was a deplorable fact, since the country was at present 'staking its all in defence of Christian principles'. A country parson had been shocked to find that a majority of the evacuee school-children under his care did not know why they were cele-brating Christmas. The author's next comments are particul-arly revealing, reflecting as they do a conservative grudge against the expenditure of taxpayers' money, a total blindness to the realities of life in the big cities both before and during the war, its poverty, deprivation and danger, but, on the other hand, a pious Christian concern for the saving of souls rather than mere vulnerable bodies. 'If that patient beast of burden, the British taxpayer, feels inclined to grumble later at the bill for the expenses of Evacuation, he may console himself with the thought that "the greatest Exodus since Moses" has had some unexpected and useful results', that is, it had been brought home to unduly complacent and 'comfortable' citizens that a considerable section of the younger generation 'has been allowed to grow up in an environment lacking many of the social decencies and amenities which most of them take for granted. It has also made it abundantly clear, even to the most short-sighted citizen, that, despite the much-vaunted excellencies of our educational system, we have somehow or other failed to ensure that more than a comparatively small proportion of the boys and girls of England are being "Christianly and virtuously brought up" with a sound knowledge of those spiritual truths which, in the language of the Catechism, "a Christian ought to know and believe to his soul's health".'

For many practising Christians the war was somehow seen as a conflict between Good and Evil, in which ultimate victory would depend on our moral Christian fibre as much as on tanks and planes. 'If God be for us—who can be against us?' was the text chosen by the Baptists in one of their regular newspaper advertisements. That was in August 1940. But obviously God could not be relied on to help us win if our children were no better than little heathens and our adults turned our towns and cities into something not much better than Sodom and Gomorrah. In the June 1940 issue of the parish magazine the vicar wrote:

His Majesty the King has called the Nation to Prayer next Sunday; I want to write a word about this Call to Prayer, because it must be sustained.

1. It must be commenced with penitence. It is well to remember that what we call our National sins are sins committed by individuals. We become so used to seeing or committing or reading about these common sins that we lose the sense of our horror of sin. Yesterday there was a long list of the names of those who had died to save their King and Country, and in the very next column there was a longer list of those who had been divorced; every one of those names meant that either husband or wife had been false to their marriage promises, and very many had committed the sin of adultery.

For every bedroom sin, is the implication, a life is sacrificed on land, sea, or in the air. An ancient, primitive stirring of guilt.

The author of the article in the *Standard* had argued that, in a country 'staking its all in defence of Christian principles' religious instruction could not be left to the Churches, since this 'encourages the fallacy that essential education can be completely secular' when in fact 'religion must form the very basis of any education worth the name.' And yet religious instruction was compulsory in all state schools, and was rigidly enforced. Every morning started off with the ritual gabble of prayers and hymns in general assembly, after which we were marched off to our classrooms for the ritual chant of multiplication tables. As a foreign heathen I managed to pick up the Lord's Prayer bit by curious bit, listening to the other children recite it daily in singsong voices, heads bowed, hands together, eyes screwed up tight but cheating, peeping, but the meaning confused me, and it took me much longer to find out who Jesus was. When I finally did I felt acutely ashamed and embarrassed. You see, there was this carol about the little lord Jesus sleeping with the stars up above him, no crib for a bed. And then I had seen an issue of the comic *Dandy*, where on the front page, I saw a black cat lying in a hammock under a night sky full of stars. So I naturally assumed . . .

7

FOR me the death of Chamberlain and my mother's embarrass-
ment in case the farmer's wife, down below in her kitchen,
should have heard my small brother let out his mistaken hooray,
emphasised that we were foreign. As such we were constantly on
probation, watched, open to criticism. It was important not to
say or do the wrong thing, or draw attention to oneself. Above
all, one must never be heard speaking one's own language,
which had become that of the enemy. It was all right to outdo
the other children on the playground by yelling *Donner und
Blitzen, Achtung* or *Heil Hitler*, the odd phrases picked up from
the radio and particularly, since the war, radio comedians,
but no more. The language of childhood had become the
tongue of lunatics and maniacs, and a sort of mental curtain
came down, dividing this from intimate exchange, lyric and
song, which had to stay secret and hidden. Children strutted
and goosemarched round the playground, making spluttering,
guttural noises which were supposed to sound like German.
Sometimes, when I heard Hitler making one of his hysterical
speeches on the radio, heard his distorted speech with its
curious vowels and consonants, I felt the playground view of
German had some validity, because he sounded so peculiar and
I could hardly understand a word. My mother explained that
he was Austrian, and they spoke what was almost a different
language. Still, he did sound decidedly comical. He *was* funny,
like the radio comedians made out. But when, after our move
to Cirencester, Chaplin's *The Great Dictator* ran at the Picture
House during the winter and I asked to see it, my mother said
'No, Hitler is not funny.'

But there was something more about the death of Chamberlain which, by some curious osmosis, had permeated into our young consciousness, something ambivalent: my mother was embarrassed, but not sorry, in fact she laughed when she told my brother to hush in case anyone heard. Somehow, in conversation heard, or overheard, the name must have acquired the overtones of a villain, even if he was British. Adult argument had impinged that far on our awareness.

That British feelings were still muddled and divided on the subject of Chamberlain by the time he died, even though the war had started, or because it had started anyhow, is made manifest in an obituary poem published in the local *Standard*, curious in its ambivalence:

> 'Hail and farewell!' we dared to say
> To your true Spirit passed away;
> We hailed you as a Saviour then—
> A Man amongst the common men.
> The raiding claim is answered now
> And every hand is at the plough:
> Had you not kept the wolf at bay
> Things would be different to-day.
> We glory in the race you ran.
> You perfect English gentleman!
> —S. McH.

'Things' could hardly have been worse for Britain at the time this was written, but the ultimate defence was that he had behaved like an English gentleman, and Hitler had not. Others might of course argue that a man who tries to do a deal with a gang of robbers and murderers is no gentleman. The arguments continued.

Meanwhile every hand was at the plough—that is, every farmhand who had not been called up. Gloucestershire farmers had set an enthusiastic example, ploughing by moonlight in the spring of 1940. At a meeting of the N.F.U. in the Corn Hall local farmers were congratulated on ploughing up more land than in any other area of Gloucestershire, 'and probably more than any area in the country'. But the speaker warned that it was important for workers to call themselves 'cowman' or 'general farm labourer', rather than 'dairymen' and 'hedge cutters', or they would be in danger of getting called up.

In the same week as the farmers of Cirencester were being congratulated for ploughing up nearly 7,000 acres, the local paper announced that Lord Bathurst's hounds would be taking part in the first two meets of the season, fixed for the coming week, whilst the Duke of Beaufort had five meets coming up in the next seven days. The same issue of the *Standard* mentioned that Alison Nairn, M.A. had produced a useful booklet entitled 'Feeding Dogs in Wartime', but it was not suggested that she had anything as ambitious as the Bathurst or Beaufort hounds in mind. In the same week the Ministry of Food announced that the full meat ration for adults would be 1s 10d per week, and 11d for young children.

The death of Chamberlain coincided with the start of yet another foxhunting season, and perfect English gentlemen once more gathered for the traditional rite of keeping the local fox at bay. Strange, almost bizarre, but true.

When I first examined my memories of Cirencester there was one image which my adult reason refused to credit even though the vivid picture was indelibly recorded on the retina of my mind's eye: looking through the lodge gates which opened on to the Tetbury Road, on one of our regular school walks, to see the Bathurst hounds barking and yelping on the grass outside their long row of kennels. I asked about them, because I had never seen so many dogs together, and got an explanation. But in spite of this clear recollection my rational mind rebelled: how could I have seen a pack of hounds baying for meat through the gates to the park, when we walked along the Tetbury Road in the summer of 1941? It did not seem possible.

But it was possible. My memory had not been playing tricks. The records of the British Library in London more than confirmed my hallucination. It seems that, by November 1940, when Britain and the whole of Europe faced a grim winter, even the *Wiltshire and Gloucestershire Standard* of Cirencester felt that some explanation was called for, however pleased they were to announce the start of a new foxhunting season:

That this should be so when we are engaged as we are at the present time may appear somewhat puzzling to the many strangers in our midst. But there are reasons in plenty why hunting should go on, due regard being paid—as certainly it will be—to the wartime difficulties of the farmer. It will show how little Hitler has affected British morale. It will refresh the 'air-tired' pilots of the R.A.F. and Army and Navy officers on leave as no other form of relaxation could. It will keep down the number of foxes. Also—far more important than all these—it will keep alive a sport which, in a district like this, is little short of an 'essential industry'. The ramifications of foxhunting are so many and so wide that it is difficult to see who, in an agricultural district, fails to benefit, directly or indirectly, from this sport. There will come a day when we shall have put the Nazi and Fascist gangsters where they belong—when the now flourishing war industries will suddenly flop . . . and in the day of 'this freedom' we shall need the outlet of every source of employment available. A pack of hounds, like Rome, is not built in a day, nor could the deepest purse make good in one or a dozen seasons the defects which would exist in a pack which had been allowed to 'go to the dogs'.

A vision of England where nothing had changed, and nothing would change, once the foreign gangsters had been disposed of. Even at the age of eight I had seen more than this local journalist: piles of rubble and ruined streets round the untouched dome of St. Paul's. The sight might have given him a different vision of postwar priorities, but it was a whole world away.

* * *

I was disappointed when I heard that we were to leave the farmhouse, but I did not attempt to dissuade my mother from making a move, because I felt it would make no difference. I had spent a good deal of time puzzling over her dissatisfaction with a place that had given me so much pleasure, and came to the conclusion that my mother was committed to the depths of her soul to modernity: hygiene, clean pale cream walls and electric switches, and that the sounds and smells of the old-fashioned farmhouse, the oil lamps, dark woodwork, cowpats in the lane, were anathema to her. I wished there was some way

57

of making her change her mind. The farmer's wife, who had belatedly realised that seeing off one lot of evacuees would only mean the arrival of a fresh lot, perhaps also wished she would change her mind, because she brought up a breakfast tray on our final morning. But it was too late: we were packed and ready to go.

We moved to a semi-detached house on the outskirts of the town, a pebble-dashed three up and two downer just like the rows and rows of small suburban houses we had known in London. It was a dead-end road, the house had a concrete path and a patch of scruffy, untended garden at the back. A small, prewar housing development on the very edge of the town: at the back of the garden a high grass-covered mound marked its ultimate boundary.

The house belonged to a youngish woman with one very small daughter. Her husband was away in the Forces and she moved about in a constant mood of sluggish indifference, immune to laughter or annoyance. Her hair was dyed a bright orange and she usually had a cigarette dangling from her lipsticked mouth, all of which I had been taught to recognise as signs of vulgarity in women, so I had no hesitation in suspecting her of stealing, or at least finding and keeping, a gold bracelet which I had brought from Berlin, after hunting in vain up the steep stairs to our rooms. I looked on our walks too, but it was gone, the little gold medallion my grandparents had given me. It was one of the last things they did: took me to a jeweller in a mood of smiles and secrecy to purchase a suitable chain. I had to wait near the door while they stood at the glass counter, smiling back at me, in a shop suffused by yellow electric light with the street already dark outside. Now it was lost, but I still have it with me, years after I stopped crawling up the stairs on all fours and scowling suspiciously at the landlady.

In other ways she was easy-going. She allowed us to mess about in her overgrown back yard with a minimum of fuss. We had the two large rooms upstairs and she kept herself to herself, on the ground floor. My brother and I slept in the back room, and the front room served as a sitting and dining room during the day, and became my mother's bedroom at night. Life began to follow a more normal routine. We started school.

*   *   *

I remember the first interview with Hillie in the front parlour, a room I was never to sit in again during the whole of my time at the school, since it was reserved for just such formal occasions. Hillie said her piece, while my brother and I sat in silence, staring at the gloomy walls and sombre furniture. It was not a propitious beginning. The words were hard to follow and seemed to have little to do with us. We were not drawn into the discussion. Hillie laid stress on the fact that all the children at the school had the benefit of being fed on healthy homegrown vegetables. My mother found this amusing, and we shared her laughter once we were back outside in the street, relaxed again, breathing relief after the stuffy quaintness of the sombre interview room. But she enrolled us as day pupils anyhow.

So now we were marched off each morning through the misty, wintry streets, across the railway bridge at the end of Quern's Lane, to the semi-detached Victorian villa next door to the Regal cinema for a few hours 'school'. Although that first encounter had taken place in surroundings rather less promising than a dentist's waiting room, going to school in Lewis Lane was not like school at all. It was highly enjoyable, and seemed to consist in doing things you liked doing, like reading books or singing round the piano until you felt like doing something else. Discipline was unheard of, since it was quite unnecessary: the whole school consisted of about ten children, who were more than amenable to the gentle voice of the teacher.

After my schooldays in London it was a truly amazing experience, and I could not get enough of it. At the primary school in Kingsbury, north-west London, school was rather like being in the army. A teacher blew a whistle and the children rushed from all corners of the asphalt playground to form up in lines. Talking was not allowed, and if the teacher was feeling particularly severe he or she could make us wait indefinitely until the rows were not only silent but straight. Then we were marched inside with military precision in single file, watched on the playground, inspected by another teacher who stood at the entrance ('No talking, Jones—pull your socks up, *no talking*') and supervised by monitors at the head of the stairs and the length of the corridor ('Don't run, walk.')

Lessons were also carried out like a military exercise. Forty children sat in rows of double benches, girls paired with boys. Each day a large proportion of the morning was devoted to chanting the multiplication tables out loud, all twelve of them. Reading involved learning poems off by heart—on one occasion we had to learn 'The Lady of Shalott' in groups of two on a bench, each bench being assigned one verse. As the first pair sat down, the two children on the bench behind stood up to recite the next verse, whilst the teacher used her ruler like a conductor's baton.

She also used it to painful effect on the knuckles of children who got out of line. More serious offenders, invariably boys, were sent upstairs to be caned by the headmaster, who was no ogre, but a gentle little man called Smith who was merely doing his duty. He did not cane girls, but gave them a kindly 'talking to', to make them see the error of their ways. Even 'games' were carried out with military precision: we were divided up into teams wearing bands of varying colours and rushed up and down in lines to the frequent sound of the teacher's whistle. Needless to say I never learnt anything in this atmosphere.

After the vast modern complex surrounded by asphalt, wired off from the main road down below, the roomy Victorian villa in Lewis Lane seemed like a home from home. It was peaceful, and relaxed. No marching in single file, no physical training in vest and knickers. Zoë and Hillie spoke to each child as an individual. Neither of them was ever heard to shout, blow a whistle, or discipline a child with a ruler, let alone a cane. Nor did the other children present a threat: since there were so few of them there was no ganging up, on each other, or on me. Instead of row upon row of desks, messy with lumpy ink from clogged inkwells, and fixed benches, a long communal room overlooking the garden, chairs round a table, two upright pianos opposite the open fireplace, bookshelves full of stories along the wall opposite the tall window with the verandah beyond.

Real books, that was perhaps the most important of many discoveries which made that semi-detached Victorian villa a turning point in my life. In our state primary school back in London we had been issued with graded readers. Once a week the school 'library' opened, stacks of books laid out on an upstairs landing, and we could choose from a tattered collection of pulp as uninspired as the compulsory readers through which the more backward pupils, almost always boys, stumbled painfully, hesitating over words of more than one syllable, ears reddening in agony as silence grew to shame and fear. Would it be humiliation or punishment, sarcasm or the ruler?

But at Arkenside books were a pleasure, not a necessary obstacle course to get through life. Nobody required us to read out loud, nobody had to, because we could not wait to turn the page and find out what happened next. That is the fundamental difference between a reader and a book. Zoë and Hillie believed in books, and they let us loose to pick and choose at will amongst a treasure house of good stories intended for no particular age group, or all of them. Kipling and Arthur Ransome, magic pillar boxes, fairies, school stories, Hiawatha, Puck coming out of Pook's Hill, and first hints of Shakespeare.

In the intimate atmosphere of a small group of children no one was ever publicly humiliated by having to stumble over unfamiliar words. Nobody ever had to read out loud, or was tested publicly on their sums either, or any other subject. It was always assumed that each child could do anything it was set to do, and later—when the attic room had been converted into a schoolroom for serious work—children of different ages worked quietly on their own, getting on with sums, making a start on French at the age of nine, or drawing buttercups for nature study. It is true that when the sums happened to turn out wrong, or when I got hopelessly confused by the mysteries of French verbs, one was apt to be made to feel, at least by Zoë, that this somehow indicated a failure of character, of moral fibre and persistence on one's own part, since my intelligence was taken for granted. But this lamentable falling away from the standard expected of me remained a secret between the two of us, and when I finally grasped and mastered the difficulty without assistance. I felt like a soul redeemed. Plump sister Hillie was much softer and more indulgent, we were all her babies, whilst the only other teacher, a tall and bony woman called Miss Betts, was neither soft nor stern, she merely supervised, calmly made ticks and crosses in one's exercise book without comment or explanation, warmth or censure.

But above all the lack of regimentation was bliss. No crass learning by rote, no period bells, whistles, no marching about, no running round in vest and knickers, inhaling dust from a floor still strewn with bits of potato from the school dinner, the boiled-cabbage smell still hanging in the air, to the sound of a voice and piano coming from the wireless. In London we had done a lot of work from the wireless, schools broadcasts on music, for example. And then there were film shows of plants growing in speeded up motion, which, combined with the dark, the comparative lack of discipline, and the constant possibility of mechanical failure, made for a good deal of hilarity, a whispering and giggling made more hectic both by the cover which the darkened hall provided and the pent-up high spirits too long held in check in the classroom.

But Zoë and Hillie did not go in for new-fangled teaching methods like the wireless. In the London primary school making music meant banging away in a percussion group, but the sisters' notion of music-making, so central to their lives, derived from the Edwardian drawing room of their childhood. Hillie played the flute, Zoë the piano, and sometimes, on a Sunday afternoon, once I had become a boarder, they would give us little recitals in their private sitting room, which had a grand piano.

Apart from singing round the piano, all the children were encouraged to take piano lessons, which for me began as sheer happiness but soon became an object of terror, faced with my growing sense of ineptitude and Zoë's stern impatience, so that I came to dread the lessons. Practising alone was more fun, and there was always a mad scramble to get to the better of the two upright pianos, after which one banged away, trying to drown out the sound of the other child playing an entirely different piece.

On the landing next to the bathroom an old spinet stood in a state of dusty disuse behind a velvet curtain. I peered at it occasionally, and hoped one of the sisters would bring it back to life, but it remained silent.

No film shows either, in spite of the fact that the school was hemmed in between the town's only two cinemas. Once I had become a boarder, in the following term, long afternoon walks down country lanes and up the Broad Ride of Cirencester Park became the basis and background of nature study. So did the garden, which by the summer of 1941 housed chickens, rabbits and a beehive, and also had a walled vegetable garden at the bottom.

A three-dimensional living world instead of a shadowy thin shoot sprouting jerkily across the flickering screen until the projector broke down and someone had to turn on the lights and help the teacher wind the spilling celluloid back on to the spools. Books became three-dimensional too, when Hillie read aloud to us, or Miss Betts, once tea and homework was finished and the sky was growing dark above the lime tree outside. And as though that was not enough, we performed bits quite often. I played the Mad Hatter round the tea-table once, and unintentionally memorised an entire scene for the rest of my life.

*   *   *

We celebrated my mother's birthday in November 1940 with a cake and several candles, luckily not one for each year, in the upstairs front room of the semi-detached, at a table which overlooked the empty road. It was a quality of suburban life in those days that, apart from stray children and dogs, the odd bicycle and the milkman, the streets were always deserted, and the few roads round the house in which we were now billeted were the nearest thing to a London suburb, although a miniature version. You had only to walk down Cotswold Avenue, which had the solidity and permanence of an earlier era of residential building, with mature gardens (one exotic with pampas grass) to be back in the town itself.

My mother did not much care for icing, which my brother and I consumed between us. When it was all gone I started nibbling at one of the rosette candleholders, and discovered that it crumbled under my teeth, and tasted saccharine sweet. I told my brother of my great discovery, that the candleholders were edible, and we ate them up between us. Shortly afterwards we were both sick. My mother put us to bed in the back room.

It would have been a boring end to the afternoon if the tedium had not been broken by the sound of gunfire. We started bouncing about on the beds, peering out at the grey sky. Life had been very quiet since we arrived in Cirencester: this was more like the old days. Our expert ears told us that the ack-ack had scored a direct hit, and judging from the direction of the noise the Jerry plane must have come down in the park. We let out a cheer for our side, duly elated, though sorry to be cooped up in bed at such a moment.

We saw the wreckage next day. It had landed just inside the park gates, on the grass verge of the Broad Ride. Several people were standing round it, peering at the crumbled heap of broken metal. We stood and stared for a bit, and I was overcome by a feeling of appalled horror, because the main body of the plane, where the airmen had been sitting, was smashed and twisted. For the first time I began to apprehend the war, not as a kind of football match between Them and Us, but as a game which involved death. It came home to me that Germans, too, were flesh and blood, and I hardly dared to think how mutilated the airmen inside the plane had been if the impact with earth had done so much damage to solid machinery. I peered anxiously for signs of death, bits of human body, or blood, but saw nothing in the wrecked cockpit, peeled open like an old tin can. I was done with cheering, and yesterday's triumph, any initial excitement at seeing the broken wings with their black crosses flattened into a patch of English grass, quickly died away, overcome by thoughts which I kept to myself.

*   *   *

It was a turning point, this incident, in my attitude to the war, and made a deep and lasting impression on me. That an incident in peaceful Cirencester, the only one that occurred during my entire stay, should have had this effect is odd. But perhaps not so odd. In London one was too much in the thick of it, directly threatened, living in constant fear as the walls shook and the sirens wailed, taking the bottom of one's stomach with it, to have any thoughts, let alone sentiment, left over for the enemy.

Of course, I could have been wrong on this particular occasion, and the Germans had perhaps bailed out. The incident was not recorded in the local newspaper, because of the censorship restrictions. But only a couple of weeks before the plane came down in the park, the *Standard* had published an article about German airmen bailing out over the English countryside, and told local farmers what to do if they found a German pilot wandering about in their fields.

The tone of the article is relaxed, as befits a small country town which was never to have a single casualty from air attack in six years of war. It is also anecdotal, and confirmed the popular view that the assurance of ultimate victory lay in England's moral superiority. Some of the German airmen, it seems, expressed themselves relieved and happy to be out of it all. But England's superiority was at all times felt to be more than merely moral. It had something to do with character, a sense of humour, and the capacity to produce and imbibe cups of tea in a crisis. It is fittingly encapsulated in the story of two women who met a German airman wearing an iron cross. 'Are you going to shoot me?' he asked in good English. 'No,' answered one of the women. 'We don't do that in England. Would you like a cup of tea?'

*　*　*

For a small country town like Cirencester the Battle of Britain was happily remote. It meant an inconvenient increase in the influx of evacuees, and the late arrival, by September, of the London papers. As a contribution to the battle of the skies a subscription list for the purchase of a Cirencester Spitfire, to be presented to the R.A.F. was opened in August 1940. 'The cost of these nippy little fighters,' reported the *Standard*, 'which have struck such deep terror into the hearts of the Nazis is generally put at £5,000.' Not a large sum for even a small town, particularly as its population had substantially increased because of the war. But the Spitfire Fund had to compete with a flourishing National Savings campaign, which was doing very well by the summer of 1940, and it never really got off the ground. By September 7th the fund stood at £224, by September 14th, on the eve of the peak of the Battle of Britain, the fund had reached £366, and by the 28th of the month it was still only £565. The following week a rather desperate advertisement appeared in the local paper, announcing that the Spitfire Fund 'only' required another £4,391 to send the town's nippy little fighter on its way. By October 26th it had reached £760, and two days before the deadline there was still £4,023 4s 3d to be raised somehow. The New Zealand Foresters gave a tree-felling exhibition in the grounds of the Abbey which raised £57, and eight hundred people watched Reg Grundy, twice world champion, win all the competitive events. In November a total of £1,375 12s 7d was sent to Lord Beaverbrook as Minister for Aircraft Production, and a town surrounded by airfields never quite managed to fly its very own plane.

8

CHRISTMAS in Cirencester was my first ordinary, mundane Christmas. The dazzling blur of my very early Christmases in Berlin had gone for good, the endless vistas of expensive toys in a city ablaze with illuminated trees.

But I enjoyed it nevertheless. It stands out in my memory as the year we adopted the English custom of having a stocking at the end of the bed, probably for the very good reason that the presents were few in number, small and cheap that year. We savoured the absence of adults, whispering and fumbling in the dark at five o'clock in the morning. I had got what I wanted, a pocket torch complete with battery. Perhaps my mother assumed I wanted it for walking in the blackout, the usual reason for acquiring one in those days, and for the scarcity of batteries. In fact I needed one so that I could read under the bedclothes, and thought myself remarkably cunning, and my mother very obtuse, for having given me what I wanted, when I intended to use it to disobey her. Throughout the war I continued to ruin my eyesight by reading under the bedclothes, until the air-raid warning sounded and I hastily hid book and torch before my mother came to rouse me. Once we had taken shelter from possible flying glass in the hallway I would have another chance to read, unless the guns got too noisy, or the neighbours arrived, or my drowsy brother started his annoying habit of dozing off and keeling over the page I was reading.

But when, after Christmas, I became a boarder at Arkenside, there was no reading under the bedclothes. I do not know why. Perhaps the battery had run out, or my mother had taken the torch back to London. Perhaps I simply did not dare, knowing that someone in the dormitory would 'tell' if I began to indulge in unlawful pleasures under the bedclothes. If I got under the bedclothes it was only in a fruitless effort to keep warm. Once warm, my chilblains began to itch. I rubbed and rubbed, trying to ignore my stomach growling with hunger.

It was my idea that I should become a boarder. Or perhaps she suggested it and I said yes, I would like it. Anyhow, my mother seemed to fall in with the idea so quickly that it must have presented itself to her as the solution to the problem of long-term evacuation. My brother was too young to know his own mind, though he was docile enough during the first few days. It was when he came to find me alone, in the hour after nightfall, just before bedtime, and told me he was homesick, starting to cry, that I got furious with him for being a ninny. He had triggered something off in me, and I found myself choking back a wave of misery as I watched him snivel. I had been doing fine until that moment, not at all homesick. I had been so proud of my new independence, my status as a boarder that when, during the first few days, we were marched out for our afternoon walk and encountered my mother, who had not yet gone back to London, on the pavement opposite the school, I felt quite resentful and would have preferred not to see her. The little crocodile stopped, Zoë spoke to her, summoned me forward to say hello to my mother. I sulked. What was the good of being a boarder if the first person you met when you stepped out of the door was your own mother? Why didn't she go home, as she had intended to do? A few months later I would have been thankful to see her, if only to still the gnawing hunger for a few hours.

Because our little paradise proved to have one serious drawback: we did not get enough to eat. As the months went by we all became increasingly obsessed with food, and most of us would have lied, cheated or stolen for a morsel of bread. During morning break we were each given a small green apple to eat on the verandah, and we ate the core. Once my brother, delegated to feed the chickens, tasted some of their grub. The teachers and their adopted toddler, who was extremely fat, sat at a separate table, with toast in a toast rack. If it was burnt to a cinder and inedible, pupils were allowed to eat it. It tasted like charcoal. Zoë and Hillie would smile indulgently at our odd taste in food. I do not think it occurred to them that we were just plain hungry. All the time. The worst time was early evening, since there was no meal after tea, which consisted of one slice of bread and margarine, with a little jam. Although we were sent to bed early, it was not early enough to stop our stomachs growling. Occasionally we were sent to bed with a lump of sugar or a cube of cheese no bigger than a sugar lump, and we would suck this as slowly as possible to make it last.

For all the 'goodness' of homegrown vegetables in the walled kitchen garden, which Hillie had recommended in that first interview, in spite of the chicken run and the beehive which would produce its first honey harvest the following summer, we began to show signs of malnutrition. Once a day we lined up at the scullery door and Hillie pushed a spoon of nauseating, glutinous cod liver oil and malt into each mouth in turn, but it could not make up for our meagre diet. I began to suffer from chilblains which, by the following winter, had become a torment as the itching red skin of my swollen fingers broke and made piano lessons quite impossible. Apart from this discomfort I remained in good health during that year, but my brother began to look increasingly peakish. He wilted, looked pale, came out in boils. The sisters took him to see a doctor, who ordered him to have regular sun-ray treatment. Eventually my mother took him back home, where he ate his way steadily back to health.

We spent a good deal of our waking hours thinking about food. Letters home were full of hints, but though our parents were generous with food parcels, in spite of rationing, it did no good: these treasure chests were not only shared out amongst all the pupils, which was fair enough, but dished out instead of our regular diet, so we stayed hungry. A walk in autumn in Cirencester Park meant the chance to forage for beechnuts in the fallen leaves, tiny crumbs of nutrition in triangular concave brown shells which all too often revealed little more than bits of fibre.

Visits from parents meant food. Our hearts were unashamedly in our stomachs. One day my father, who was no longer stationed in the town, unexpectedly stood on the front doorstep in his heavy boots and khaki battledress. The left breast pocket promised chocolate. He always kept his ration for us. He got permission to take us out for the afternoon and we stuffed ourselves in the tea rooms of Ann's Pantry, near the Market Place. We sat among the brown Windsor chairs and checkered table clothes and my father laughed as he ordered more, and more again, at the way we stuffed ourselves. Strangers at neighbouring tables joined in the laughter as the waitress came back with more portions of toast and cakes. When he was in a good mood my father had a way of sharing his high spirits with anyone who happened to be in the vicinity. Normally we found this an embarrassing trait, but on this occasion we were much too busy pacifying the growling beast inside us to care who saw us, or who laughed. That night, shortly after we had been put to bed, my brother was violently sick. One of the sisters came to tell me what had happened. She also gave me a little moral lecture on my responsibilities as an older sister: I should not have allowed him to make a pig of himself.

The obsession with food took many forms. We would lie awake in the dormitory at night, stomachs rumbling, and discuss our favourite dishes, invent imaginary menus. My friend Isolde, whose temperament combined intelligence with cunning, was not inclined to take refuge in fantasy. I had already found her once, hovering suspiciously near a biscuit tin in the basement kitchen, which must once have been the servants' room. She had bright red pigtails and would blush furiously under her ginger freckles when caught in the act. As though this was not enough, she had the singular habit of humming long and tunelessly under her breath when she knew herself guilty. The biscuits, I said in a righteous tone, belonged to Joyce. They had been sent by her mother. I resisted any suggestion of bribery, by sharing the spoils.

One afternoon we were assembled in the area basement in our outdoor clothes, ready for the afternoon walk, when Zoë addressed us with unusual sternness. Apparently a 'mouse' had been in the scullery. This creature had eaten part of a cake, but instead of simply cutting a slice, it had tried to hide its nefarious deed by nibbling all round the cake, making it unfit for human consumption. Unless the mouse person owned up, there would be no jam for a week. Nobody spoke, though everyone knew who was responsible. We stood waiting while Isolde hummed like a hive of bees, her mouth firmly shut in case one of them should escape, her complexion now a deep beetroot. Nobody spoke. Nobody did more than glance at Isolde. Nobody had jam for a week.

But Isolde's sly cunning could also benefit us all on occasion. One summer afternoon she and I were playing together on the lawn when she said suddenly, with affected innocence, so loudly that Zoë, who was only a yard away, could not fail to hear: 'Have we had tea?' Zoë duly overheard, and was so shocked at the inadequacy of our first tea that she immediately ordered a second one for everybody. Isolde was triumphant at the success of her ruse. But unfortunately it had no lasting effect. It proved what I have always suspected, that it was not war scarcity, or parsimony, that made us hungry: the two maiden sisters with their delicate appetites and lack of experience as mothers simply had no conception of how much growing youngsters needed in the way of nourishment, though their adopted little girl, the pet of the school, was podgy enough. On that memorable summer afternoon Isolde's cunning worked: we were given a second tea. But by the following day our rations were back to normal.

But the most memorable feast day of all was the afternoon when Isolde's mother and stepfather, a major in the army, arrived on a visit. Instead of taking her out, they brought food back—for the whole school. Excitement reached fever pitch as they took our orders for cakes, with mountains of cream buns an easy favourite. Laughing, they made out a list, hardly able to make out what we were saying because everyone was talking at once. I could not believe they would come back, it was too much like those night fantasies. Zoë and Hillie would never allow it. But the two sisters did nothing to prevent it, though it might have offended their puritan principles. They kept out of the way that afternoon, perhaps overawed by the major's crowns, and in due course Isolde's tall slim mother and the rather

71

tubby, genial major returned, all smiles and packages and paper bags. They must have cleaned out every cake shop in town.

* * *

Isolde was my best friend. She could read very thick books with tiny print, like *Lorna Doone*, for instance, whose ramifications of plot and paragraph were beyond me. She had brains and cunning and a ruthless streak which made her a sparring partner, a friend who was always a potential enemy. She had a subdued younger sister, the same age as my brother, whom she regarded as a pathetic ninny if she came for protection or comfort. Her sister spent most of the first term looking lost and miserable but, just as I was angry with my brother for crying, we affected to ignore the poor kid's unhappiness.

Isolde and her sister had a German father from whom their mother was divorced. He was still in Germany, and we understood that he had chosen to stay in Germany, a case of divided loyalty. Her mother's patriotism was not in doubt, since she had a nice British major to prove it, and I suppose divorce and remarriage, an unusual event in those days, may have been simplified by the war, not its cause, in that it provided an explanation for the children.

It was Isolde who unwittingly inflicted a mortal wound on me. Thinking back now, I wonder whether I was not at least partly responsible. Or all of us, as a group. With hindsight it is easy to see that Isolde must have had her own wounds, with a German father who was fighting on the other side. We would all have regarded him as a Nazi. But Isolde did not show wounded feelings, her temperament was to brazen things out; on the defensive, she would attack. For years I held her father, his indoctrination, responsible for what she said: thinking back now, I realise that her father was the cause, but not in the way I thought.

One night in the dormitory, as we mumbled our usual bedtime prayers under the bedclothes, she told me I could stop saying mine right away. I did not believe in God anyhow. Indignantly I protested my faith. Of course I believed in God.

72

No, she said, she had heard that I was a Jew and Jews did not believe in God.

I lay awake and miserable, staring into the dark. Please God, I said in an anxious whisper, don't take any notice of her. I do believe in you. But I was also bewildered and puzzled. How could other people know things about me that I did not know myself? I had never heard the word Jew before, and I did not know what it meant.

I carried my misery round like a stone in my stomach. For days. I took to locking myself in the basement lavatory, the only private place in the house. I stared at the small patch of sky visible through the high window, and thought perhaps that my grandmother, who would have comforted me, was looking at exactly the same sky that covered us both, though she was so far away in Germany and I could no longer reach her.

When it came to writing the weekly letter home I told my mother that I was very unhappy and that I wanted to come home. Isolde had said that I did not believe in God. The following morning I was told that Zoë wanted to see me. She was sitting down in the basement with my letter in her hand. She told me that Isolde was a very naughty girl to say such wicked things, and that she would talk to her. On the other hand, my mother had a lot of worries on her mind, and I would only make her more worried with a letter like this. 'Now go away and write another letter.'

It was my first experience of censorship. It had not occurred to me that the teachers read our letters home. Although mollified by Zoë's tone of voice, I also felt trapped. I could not think what to say in the second letter, and wrote a brief, meaningless note that said nothing at all. I kept a careful watch on Isolde for a day or two, hoping to see her duly chastened, but she showed no signs. If she had been rebuked she was careful to appear nonchalant and happy as she played with other children, not me. But that was like her.

The matter was closed. Nobody ever spoke of it again. Only for me it was not closed, for years the wound rankled in my mind. I had thought of myself as a unique human being engaged in the discovery of myself. The sheltered schooling I

73

now enjoyed had encouraged self-discovery: for the first time I was not an appendage of my parents, part of a family unit, or part of a huge classroom where I was marshalled into conformity. I was finding out about myself, my feelings, my sensibilities. I had fallen in love with words and begun to write short poems and stories. The people who took care of me were educators with a sense of values to which I could respond. I could also respond to their affection, which was based on clear-sighted recognition and left me oddly free, responsible for my own actions. Now it seemed that I did not know myself at all, or at least that the world had a label for me which I did not understand, which flatly contradicted everything I knew about myself. How was this possible? Was it like a secret disease, something under the skin, in my blood, which I did not know about? Zoë had said that Isolde was naughty, but not that she was mistaken. I had been vindicated, but nothing was explained. The puzzle of identity remained at the back of my mind. I suppose it has been there all my life. The question 'What is a Jew?' is familiar enough. For me it began in the dormitory at Arkenside.

9

THE two sisters were as different as chalk from cheese, but they complemented each other. Zoë was the elder, and it was obvious even to a small child that she was in control, that her sister, although middle-aged, was somehow still soft, the baby of the family. Zoë was in command, she was the organiser, and Hillie would undoubtedly turn to her for instructions not just in a crisis, but several times a day.

Father had been some sort of army officer in the previous war, and his sepia photograph hung in the boys' dormitory; I imagined the woman they referred to as 'mother' as being more like Hillie, soft and ladylike, who indulged the baby of the family and played music in the drawing room, perhaps the disused spinet behind the curtain on the first-floor landing. Zoë could have commanded an army with assurance, and if the soldiers had all been like me, they would have gone over the top and died with adoration in their hearts, for her, not king and country.

Hillie was plump, a cushion to lean on, with a face like soft white bread. Zoë, on the other hand, was small and wiry, with features all bone and sharp definition. She moved briskly through the day, her finely beaked nose like a prow, firm forehead, strong chin, greying hair neatly bobbed for a minimum of fuss. Zoë did not like fuss, or indecision, or unnecessary whining. In any one day she would get through an immense variety of small tasks with the same attack and brisk down-to-earth practicality, whether it was beekeeping, organising the school, or giving a music lesson, which precluded any notion of incompetence or failure. Things had to be done, and Zoë did them. With a war on, Zoë had not only moved and reopened the school in a strange town, within no time at all she started work on the vegetable garden, with children weeding in their spare time, and set up a chicken run, some rabbit hutches, and a beehive. She prepared buckets of chicken feed, and children were delegated to feed them, or let them out for a run on the long lawn. Nobody needed to be asked to feed lettuce leaves to the rabbits or count the babies. But only Zoë, gloved and helmeted like a gladiator, dared to tackle the bees. I watched her working on the hive once, and a bee tangled in my hair and I got stung on the scalp. As she took me back to the house, sniffling with pain and self-pity, for treatment, Zoë gave me one of her little moral lectures. *I* might have a sore head, but the poor bee who had stung me was now dead. It was not that Zoë felt no sympathy for my suffering, but she believed in teaching a sense of proportion. Walking up the garden path, I thought about the bee whose death I had provoked by getting my hair in its way.

There was something hawk-like about her face, shrewd without being predatory. Her deep-set eyes missed nothing, but were saved from severity by a constant tendency to twinkle, and the deeply etched lines of humour which radiated from the corners. She did not coo and cluck like her soft-hearted, sentimental sister, who had a taste for baby-talk and a tendency to anthropomorphise the birds and the bees. Any personal comment was more likely to be a brisk admonition, and praise was rare. She saw, not a child or a baby, but a human being capable of doing anything he or she set her mind to. If I did less, I was letting her down. Which was why I would gladly have died rather than fail her.

I did let her down rather badly over my piano lessons. Very soon after I became a boarder it had been suggested to my mother that I would benefit from music lessons. There was nothing exceptional about this, since the sisters worked on the principle that all their pupils should learn to play an instrument. But although I was at first very excited at the notion of playing the piano, my initial enthusiasm turned to bewildered dismay as I progressed through the graded pieces and found myself required to play more than one note at a time. Two hands doing two different things sent me into a panic. With

76

Zoë sitting over me I got the fingering wrong, and was rewarded each time with a painful rap on the knuckles. This made me so nervous that more mistakes followed. Another slap on my misguided fingers. Unable to think of anything but the next blow, I counted to five out loud whilst playing four beats to the bar. By now Zoë was very cross.

I began to dread piano lessons. It never occurred to Zoë that her methods might be at fault, or that I was perhaps not unusually gifted in this direction. Because she went through life tackling a large variety of jobs with total assurance, whether it was planting cabbages, tinkering under the bonnet of a car, or teaching French verbs, she took it for granted that anyone with a grain of sense could do anything. If you failed at a particular task it meant you were simply not putting your mind to it. She once kept me up for hours, or what seemed like hours, after the other children had gone to bed: there was a concert for parents next day, and I was the only performer in a piano trio who did not know the right notes and, more important, the proper entries and pauses. She drummed the thing into me, over and over again. Tired and by now in tears, I finally got it right. Zoë took me upstairs, scrubbed me in a bath of hot clean water with a loofah, and told me, while the tears continued to stream down my face, that she had been so exacting with me because she knew I could do it. Scrubbing my skin raw with the loofah, she told me that it was because she was so fond of me, and knew me to be intelligent and gifted, that she took so much trouble with me. I must never let her—or myself—down. Red-eyed and raw-red in the steamy atmosphere, I felt infinitely privileged, and not just on account of her words. It was the privacy of the occasion. From being punished, I was now singled out, the chosen one. Having a bath to myself was an added bonus. I had missed the usual bathtime routine, in which everyone got in the same bathwater, two at a time. Since the youngest ones were scrubbed first, the water was usually tepid and disgustingly scummy by the time I was urged into it.

*　*　*

The only assistant teacher, Miss Betts, was long, gaunt and

77

bony, with a sallow complexion and a wide-angled chin above a long neck that made her look like an ostrich. She was a source of endless fascination to me, partly on account of her capacity to keep silent for long periods. She would sit with her long bony hands folded in her flat lap, quietly staring into the middle distance, her matt dark hair rolled at the base of her sallow neck, only a small pulse working at the corner of her wide jaw, as though she had been nervously chewing over the same gobbet of tough meat for so many years that she had become quite unable to swallow it. If she supervised the schoolroom she never told anecdotes, and hardly smiled. She simply sat calmly, waiting for you to bring your exercise book full of sums or your piece of sewing, waiting for the end of the afternoon. She was kind, but distant. Bad work or wrong answers provoked little comment. Unlike Zoë and Hillie, she never spoke about herself, As a result I speculated about the hidden mysteries of her existence, which I supposed to be dismally bleak. I tried to imagine the room in which she lived, what she did in her spare time, what she thought about. I speculated on the distant tragedies of her youth, but somehow it was hard to imagine even a young Miss Betts engaged in romantic dalliance. She was too tall, to begin with. I could not understand how she managed to appear so calm, and decided that she must have a firm and unshakable faith in the mysterious, superior wisdom of the Almighty. In short, I deduced that Miss Betts had resigned herself to His hands, and was living out the remainder of her days without hope, in a spirit of stoic acceptance.

If I had arrived at such a sombre, joyless view of adult religion it was due to our weekly attendance at the Methodist Church. This was a squat, ugly building near the railway station, built of red brick. Getting ready for church caused a great deal of fuss, since the sisters dressed us up for the occasion: socks had to be white, gloves had to be worn, and by the spring we had blossomed out into special Sunday frocks and panama hats. But the excitement of marching two by two in special attire ended abruptly at the porch: once we had occupied the two back pews in the right-hand corner tedium set in. The sermon seemed interminable, and the building was drearily plain. I spent a long time staring at the high unadorned windows. Tried in vain to catch a glimpse of the boy who was rumoured to be pumping air into the organ, or stared at the spot in the floor where, Joyce assured me in a whisper, people were baptised by being plunged in water from head to foot. I waited expectantly for such a sensational event to occur, but it never did. The cold, bleak little building stubbornly kept its secrets, its hidden rites.

When I revisited the building the doors were closed, inside the morning service was still going on. I waited for a bit, until I got tired of waiting. Inside I could hear a man's voice drone on, just as it had done all those years ago. Shuffling, a subdued cough. A fat woman in a blue dress was peering through the small window of the inner door, trying to see how far the service had got or who was inside. 'Are you a Methodist?' she asked, because even now, on a Sunday, everybody belongs to some denomination in a small town like Cirencester, even if they make a point of not going because they prefer a traditional Sunday lunch, with too much to eat and a family reunion. The consciousness of not going to church is still a positive force. I turned away, and left the fat woman still peering through the glass. Was I a Methodist? I had come pretty close to it once, in spite of the tedious sermons, the ugly building, in spite of being that unkown something called a Jew which had never prevented them from marching me off to church with everybody else. Not that I would have wanted to be excluded: on the contrary, I was to acquire the passion of a convert offered a land of myth, legend and moral certainties where there had been only nothingness before. I smiled at the question: are you a Methodist? Not any more, I thought, turning away down the sunny, empty street.

*　　*　　*

From small beginnings—the Old Museum erected by Lord Bathurst during the nineteenth century in the boundary wall of his estate, and no bigger than a coach house—the town now attracts tourists from all over the world as Roman Corinium. Turning the corner into Blackjack Street on our way back from the park we regularly passed by the larger museum which still stands on the same site, but for some reason Zoë never thought fit to take us inside, though I remember asking her what the building was. Since then it has been enlarged and modernised.

There is a new complex called The Forum, and the jumble of old warehouses in Lewis Lane has been cleared to make way for a parking space and a tourist information centre. The school has become a boarding house, painted a brash cream with Arkenside for a name, both houses knocked into one, a neon sign above what used to be the dentist's front door, an area of cement where the front gardens with their iron railings and shrubs had stood. Only at the back is something of the past still visible: in the neglected garden, the semi-derelict verandah stacked with rubbish, the old brick wall which had led through to the kitchen garden. But the dark red arch at the end of the footpath is filled in with newer bricks since the kitchen garden with its barn and coach house, in which the sisters' car had stood motionless for the duration of the war for want of petrol, is now separate, the site of a new bungalow. Part of the wall along the old gravel path to the back exit in The Avenue has been built into the new neat structure of the bungalow and its surrounds. The well, I was told, still stood in its garden. I tried hard, but without success, to catch a glimpse of it over the fence from the cinema car park. But the lime tree was still there, in all its glory, bigger than I remembered it. I found this surprising at first, in a world which had shrunk. But it had continued to grow in the decades since I played on the swing slung from its branches, lime blossoms dropping on to the ground, into my hair, and now it towered, a green giant of leafy splendour, over every tree and rooftop within the vicinity. It stood in triumph over time, decay and death, a living contradiction of all that I had come to expect of the sad erosion of time. It had always been a focal point of the garden, its moving green shade alive with the hum of insects; from the house, its top branches just visible from the attic window of the schoolroom, dusk gathering in its dark shape at nightfall, whispering secrets, watched from the dormitory when sleep would not come.

80

But the lawn had shrunk. The Regal cinema looked diminutive. What was left of the old council school building had been cleaned up and looked picturesque, gold, not grey. Lewis Lane had been tidied up, what was left of it; as for the house, it had lost its grey Victorian dignity and had been diligently tarted up by an owner keen on home improvements. I took a drink in the bar, walked through the carpeted space which had once been the austere front parlour where Zoë and Hillie interviewed prospective pupils and their parents, and the owner showed me where he had only recently removed a row of children's coat-pegs near the door to the verandah, three feet above floor level. The upper row, which had always been out of reach, remained. Everything had been painted cream or papered over. Only the door on to the verandah still had its border of Victorian stained glass, now partly cracked, with a piece missing.

The row of missing coatpegs recalled shoe bags, wellingtons against the dark veneered wall, cold winter mornings when damp air came through the verandah door as soon as you opened it, the sound of running feet on bare floorboards, and more pegs inside the small door which opened on to the steep, narrow staircase into the basement. This was our way out into the world, once we had our coats on: down past the kitchen into stone basement area with the lavatory in the corner and only an iron gate below the area steps. Here we assembled for our walks. The elegant front door with the hall stand beside it was reserved for visitors.

★   ★   ★

Once the damp dark winter days got longer and brighter and the air turned mild and bright the garden became a regular playground. We raced each other down the sloping lawn, poked our fingers through the wire of the rabbit hutch, and swung in the swing attached to a low strong branch of the lime tree. But the garden was more than a playground, it was a microcosm in which pleasure and instruction were combined in a way which would have been approved of by idealists of an earlier age. As each plant came into flower we learnt its name: nasturtium, geranium, larkspur, Canterbury bell. I have never owned a garden, and even now most of the names of flowers I can identify with instant assurance stem from the hours spent studying the newest, colourful calyx in the border under the verandah, whilst my knowledge of wild flowers is restricted but indelibly fixed by the walks we took in country lanes on our afternoon outings. The obscure word scabious is fixed in a hedgerow opposite an old flour mill on a stream where a small cat stalked across the grass verge, before we had been taken inside by Zoë to watch the miller at work in the dark and noisy interior, where machinery juddered as the stone wheel turned and the air was dusty with flour; each time I see the delicate azure, wild or tame, of that flower, flat as a button, petals with that slightly crumpled look, I stop and search my memory before I pull the word scabious out of the old hedge in a flat country lane long ago. It has stuck there with curious tenacity, but I tug and it comes to me in the end: an odd word for a rare flower of a blue so aloof it should have stayed up in the sky.

Meanwhile, the shaded walks under the old beeches of Cirencester Park remain littered with moss, butterwort, celandine, windflowers or wood anemones, and my very first snowdrops. We always had our eyes on the ground, shuffling among last years leaves, the husks of nuts, damp pine cones, and Zoë in particular made sure that we missed nothing and could put a name to what we saw. Later our watchful eyes were rewarded with a handful of wild strawberries.

But Zoë not only knew the names of things, she undersood their uses. Knowledge was combined with practicality, an attitude perhaps encouraged by the war, but one which must always have been fundamental to her character. If I stared into the green abundance of the lime tree with such a sense of wonder, it was partly because I had been told that you could make a sort of tea from the tiny blossoms. When, in the summer, the rabbit hutches acquired a new attraction in the shape of two splendid fluffy white angora rabbits with pink eyes, Zoë told me one sunny afternoon, as she sat on the verandah combing out the rabbits' thick white fur, that their hair was very valuable and was made into wool. I did not ask whether she would sell the fluff in the comb, but it seemed unlikely that she would throw it away. Zoë never threw anything away that could be used: she taught me how to make potato cakes from cold leftovers, and scraps of food always went into the bucket of chicken feed. No, I had no doubt that Zoë had started an angora farm, like the miniature chicken farm wired in alongside the fence and the honey factory in the beehive. At the peak of the year the golden liquid dripped into buckets on the scullery floor, and I was allowed to suck a piece of honeycomb.

But perhaps my most absorbed hours were spent in the walled vegetable garden. We were not really doing very much, just pulling up weeds and clearing the gravel footpaths between the earth beds edged with borders of dark grey flint. But it was a job after my own heart, because it allowed me to crouch and examine the minutiae of soil and gravel for what seemed like hours, picking up stones with interesting shapes, finding small shards of pottery or coloured glass which were particularly easy to find in that place. As a small child I had an instinctive archaeologist in me, and on this occasion I had come to the right place, because the spot on which I was grubbing around, pulling up chickweed and turning over stones, had once been an area of fields and gardens which had yielded the most impressive Roman remains in all Corinium, those of the palace or chief residence.

When William Stukeley came by this way more than two hundred years earlier he found the tiny town no longer filled its old Roman boundaries and fortifications. Much of the ground which had been built on by the Romans was now pasture, corn fields or gardens. 'Here they dig up antiquities every day, especially in the gardens; and in the plain fields, the track of foundations of houses and streets are evident enough.' For the locals, working in the fields and gardens, the finding of coins, mosaic floors and old ornaments was an everyday occurrence which, in the absence of experts who only arrived a century later, were treated very casually. The meadow once called the Leauses, now ordinary Lewis Lane, yielded more treasure than any other spot. By the time Stukeley arrived it had become 'one great garden called Lewis grounds', which he chose to derive from a British word for palace, *llys*. 'Large quantities of carved stones are carried off yearly in carts, to mend the highways, besides what are useful in building. A fine Mosaic pavement dug up here Sept. 1723, with many coins. I bought a little head which has been broke off from a *basso relievo*, and seems by the *tiara*, of a very odd shape, like fortification work, to have been the genius of a city, or some of the *deae matres*, which are in old inscriptions. . . . The gardener told me he had lately found a fine little brass image, I suppose one of the *lares*; but, upon a diligent scrutiny, his children had played it away.'

Who knows how much I might not have played away: probably no more than bits of Victorian crockery, but in a soil so ancient everything is mixed with everything else. The locals understand this, and have always used what they found. When Stukeley came to Cirencester the owner of the Lewis grounds, a Mr. Richard Bishop, had found vaults 'on which grow cherry trees like the hanging gardens of Babylon', and the bases of stone pillars as big in compass as his own summer house: 'these, with cornices very handsomely moulded and carved with modilions, and the like ornaments, were converted into swine-troughs: some of the stones of the bases were fastened together with cramps of iron, so that they were forced to employ horses to draw them asunder; and they now lie before the door of his house as a pavement.' When Leland arrived two hundred years before that, as a commissioner appointed by Henry VIII to investigate monastic establishments, he found that the Abbot had made use of the ruins of an old tower along the Roman fortified wall to build a new clothing mill. When the Abbey was demolished shortly afterwards the stones helped to construct the first Abbey mansion. Recently the original church font was found in the Abbey grounds, being used as a bird bath, and has now been restored to the parish church.

A respect for antiquity as something separate and special did not come until Victorian times. In May 1777, a Mr. Croome of Dyer Street was having a cellar dug under his warehouse. During the excavations an elaborate mosaic pavement was found, an affair of red interlaced hearts, blue and white chequered border, and a centrepiece formed as a star.

84

'Mr. Croome' wrote Rudder, 'had the central piece taken up, and it remained for some time entire at the entrance into the garden from his dwelling-house, where it served for part of the pavement; but being much exposed to the weather, it was gradually broken and destroyed.' But in 1837, when Mr. Brewin found a mosaic floor in his garden in Quern's Lane, he erected an ornamental house over it and allowed the public into his garden to see it.

From now on Roman finds were carefully recorded and preserved. In 1849, while a new sewer was being dug in Dyer Street, a tessellated pavement depicting hunting dogs in pursuit of vanished quarry came to light under an English sky. A month later, in September, a pavement depicting various figures of classical mythology, including Actaeon, inspired a local clergyman to rush home to his study and produce a hasty, almost impromptu translation of Ovid. By this time Professor Buckman had begun work on the many pavements that came to light and published his book on Roman antiquities in Cirencester in 1850, duly dedicated to Earl Bathurst, and with an acknowledgement to Miss Master of the Abbey 'for the facility afforded to us of examining, at our leisure, the remains of the Roman wall which passes through her grounds'. The Reverend J. Merry's translation of Ovid was also published in the volume, whilst the services of the Professor of Chemistry, a Dr. A. Voelker, at the Royal Agricultural College, recently established with the practical assistance of Earl Bathurst, were employed to analyse a small piece of glass found in the head of Flora, who wore a chaplet of ruby-red flowers made of translucent glass, once the verdigris had been removed, and was part of the most splendid find Professor Buckman could report, a pavement depicting the four seasons, although Winter was irrecoverably lost under the foundations of a house. Dr. Voelker took his job seriously: 'The following analysis of coloured glass, found at Cirencester, will enable me to present an additional proof of the great utility of chemistry in general' he wrote, and concluded that without chemical examination 'we might probably have been induced to form an erroneous opinion of the sense of harmony of colours of the Romans as exhibited in their mosaics.' But Professor Buckman had already realised that there was something odd about Flora's head when first exhumed, her chaplet consisting entirely of leaves, and as tessellae of bright green verdigris had not been found before, they started scraping the surface of these and found that 'the change from confusion to harmony was quite magical . . . the bright hue of the blossoms contrasting with the leaves, forming a floral wreath of great beauty'.

You can see it in the museum today, together with a floor depicting Orpheus surrounded by a circle of birds and a wider circle of wild beasts, though the design has been partially destroyed by the roots of a walnut tree. The digging goes on, finds carefully preserved for the tourist. The green fields are rich enough in buried history to keep archaeologists busy for years to come. But life goes on. The old warehouses and stables in Lewis Lane have been pulled down, but the old waterworks, given to the town, like everything else, by his lordship, still pumps away at the far end of Lewis Lane, near the old-fashioned flour mill which is still operating. The old brewery has been spared, but not the dark winding length of Cricklade Street, which has a gash in its side to let in a new shoppers' precinct. As for the stark Victorian dignity of the house in Lewis Lane, it has been eroded, vulgarised, adapted to a new age. In a town that continues to live, the living will continue to make swine-troughs from the remnants of yesterday. But like the people of yesterday, though they have bricked in the arch of the wall behind the lime tree, they have left it standing. If you look carefully enough, as I did, you can still trace out hints of the past.

10

I HAD some notion of the historical antiquity of the town. Somebody, perhaps Miss Betts, who walked through the town and surrounding fields and parkland like a brown ostrich, taking longer strides than anyone else, had once pointed to the pavement outside Woolworth's and remarked 'There are Roman pavements under there', so that I lived in daily expectation of finding the upper part of Cricklade Street being dug up and was surprised, as the days and weeks passed, to see shoppers and the many soldiers in the town casually walking over those few paving stones as though there was nothing remarkable about them. And another time, walking along a road near the outskirts, Zoë had said something about a Roman amphitheatre, nodding her head vaguely towards a horizon of grass and trees where there was nothing obviously remarkable to be seen, so that this ruin grew more impressive, unseen but imagined, yet remained elusive; like the source of the Thames, which was not the shallow trickle flowing between boulders under the bridge where the London road began, but somehow connected to it, flowing to meet it at a spot forever hidden in a secret mystery of rocks and leaves and overhanging branches, as though to reveal the actual spot might stop the mighty flow under London's broad bridges.

But at that age all times and places coexisted anyhow. When Hillie read out *Puck of Pook's Hill* in the attic schoolroom the idea of the past coming out of the ground seemed the most natural thing in the world. Isolde professed to be an expert on fairy rings: we discussed their attributes, and the most likely places to find them during our walks. It occurred to me that the Roman amphitheatre might be a good place to start if, like

Dan and Una, we hoped to see Roman soldiers appearing out of nowhere. But my sense of vision was very adaptable. When I read Mark Twain on the steps of the verandah the fence between me and the Regal cinema was the very one Tom Sawyer should have been whitewashing. And when I acquired and read my first Shakespeare play, *As You Like It*, the trees of Cirencester Park were instantly transformed into the Forest of Arden, and I became a lovestruck Rosalind mooning between their trunks, searching the barks for billets-doux and sighing out the few lines I could recall, which did not amount to much more than a preliminary 'oh coz' and 'sweet coz', which struck me as poetically quaint. Isolde was inclined to sneer and refused to be cast in the mould of sympathetic cousin and confidante, so I played the game on my own, losing myself in a miasma of dramatic melancholy, while she bounced away on another game, flicking her ginger pigtails. I told myself that redheads with her temperament were different, and lacked the visionary sensibility to step into the Forest of Arden, my forest.

I had acquired my own copy of *As You Like It*, small and bound in bright red cloth with gold letters on the spine, on my ninth birthday, and spent much time perusing it without any adult assistance. It had caught my eye on the shelf of the bookshop in the Market Place, where Zoë took me on the morning of my ninth birthday to purchase a Bible. I had asked for a Bible, and my mother had sent the money, also a nurse's uniform in which I was duly photographed, cradling a doll and flanked by Too-Too, the adopted toddler and school pet, my brother, and a boy with ginger freckles and fat legs called Graham. Since the Bible, illustrated with modern photographs of Palestine, only cost five shillings, I was allowed to choose something else, running my eye along the shelves behind the counter, and if I settled for *As You Like It* I must have been tempted by the miniature volume and colourful binding, guided by Zoë, and brought to a decision by a prior reading of Charles Lamb where Rosalind had been depicted in the illustration as a 1920s debutante at Ascot as she handed over her necklace. But this, I knew at once, was the real thing, and I was transported into another world, where words had a different weight, flavour and significance. It was typical of Zoë that she should have allowed, and even encouraged me to choose a Shakespearian text without in any way suggesting, that, at the age of nine, I was too young to cope with it. On the contrary, she saw me as an adult newly arrived into the world, and her task to guide me through it, pointing out things of value and interest.

I did not become an assiduous reader of the holy book, though I did spend quite a lot of time studying the photographs of the Holy Land. They intrigued me, but at the same time made the Bible stories oddly remote and Christian worship bizarre, since I could not see what England had in common with a landscape and people so utterly unlike our own. What possible connection could there be between us and weird bearded people who wore long robes and moved in a landscape of olive trees, rocks and desert, where even the houses and animals bore no relation to our own? But the small red copy of *As You Like It* opened a door. I walked straight through it and was never the same again. I was fascinated by words half understood but pregnant with more meaning than anything I had read before. In the dormitory at night I mouthed over the strange, archaic words that seemed so wonderful. For several years I wished I was called Rosalind. Long after these early impressions had been half forgotten, buried by time, I named my son Orlando.

I read in the dormitory at night because for a while I had the room to myself. My birthday, as usual, came in the Easter holiday, and it had been decided that my brother and I should not go back to London for the vacation, because of the bombing. So we remained alone in the house with Zoë, Hillie and Too-Too, in a new intimacy, more domestic, the house strangely quiet. But with no lessons, there was a danger of boredom. To start things off on the right footing Zoë asked one morning whether I could ride a bicycle. It seemed that in the old barn, which housed the black motor car for the duration of the war like a sort of mechanical Sleeping Beauty, there was also a child's Fairy cycle, below the loft where apples were laid out in long, sweet-smelling rows, skins not touching, so that one bad apple could not spoil the others.

I would have found it hard, when asked by Zoë, to admit to an inability to do anything. I said yes, I could ride a bike, too quickly, without thinking, and then thought, am I really lying? After all, I do not know, since I have never tried. Perhaps I can. Unfortunately I was now committed, and I followed her down the garden path with a growing sense of foreboding, which changed to dread as she opened the garage doors. Could I ride a bike? Any moment now I was liable to be exposed not just as a fool, an inadequate person, but also as a liar. What had possessed me to say a bald 'yes', instead of admitting that I had never tried? Now it was too late: I was trapped.

Zoë wheeled the small black bicycle along the gravel path of the kitchen garden, past the beehive, and through the brick archway to the main garden and the foot of the long lawn. I took the handlebars, and placed a tentative foot on the outside pedal. Behind me Zoë and Hillie and my brother were all waiting. I took a deep breath, hoisted myself into the saddle, and managed to ride the whole length of the upward slope without falling off. Nobody was more surprised than me. The little group behind me cheered. I risked doing it again, with equal success, and was amazed how easy it was. Life was like riding a bike, riding a bike was life. Exhilarating. When my mother came to visit us I showed off my new talent with pride, riding up and down the lawn at top speed.

My mother stood on the steps of the verandah, the sun in her eyes, and watched as I showed off my latest accomplishment, stopping the bike to yell 'Look! Watch me!' before I turned round and rode back down to the lime tree. She smiled, but her smile was wary, and I was too happy and excited to be disturbed by the slightly withdrawn look on her face as she tried so hard to share my enthusiasm. Only now, looking back, I can begin to think what that lonely year, with the whole family gone, must have been like for her.

She had begun to adapt to our new circumstances. Trained as a dressmaker because her family considered commercial art too risky a profession without something practical to fall back on, she fell back on it now. With clothes rationed, any scrap of material was turned to good use. Throughout the war there was usually a half-finished garment hanging up in the bedroom. Neighbours slipped discreetly into the bedroom while my mother mumbled through a mouthful of pins. Later she would make me up party frocks to my own specifications, which was fun, and homemade school dresses were a cut above the usual. But I was too self-conscious about my changing shape to show gratitude. Stuck full of pins, told to hold still, I stared at my image with loathing at this crude half-way stage, afraid I would look a fright, not quite daring to protest too much if I thought the result would be awful. I tried her patience, since she saw a little girl in the mirror, while I wanted to be transformed, carping and criticising, trying hard to wriggle out of my chrysalis.

It must have been a hard year for her, quite alone in that small flat, husband and children away, the strain of heavy bombing at nights. But for me it was easy, and I was too young to have developed a sense of guilt at my own disloyalty. I was happy, away from home. I revelled in my new-found sense of independence, finding things out, being a person, riding a bike as though I had grown wings. I was not homesick. If I was happy to see my parents the promise of a good square meal had as much to do with it as hugs and kisses.

Perhaps it was because, even as a very small child, I had been conscious of a secret, solitary nucleus inside which nobody could reach. It held pain, but also dreams, and I needed to be withdrawn to allow it to grow. The separateness of being away at school gave it time to grow, to find roots in friendly soil, sprout branches and blossom into the first spring of creative imagination, leaf into rapturous life, roots fed with a constant thirst for knowledge. It was only later, after the brief interlude of time and place was over, that the strains of war and its effect on my family began to impinge on me.

Not that I was cut out for community living, probably not. It was precisely because the school was small enough to make regimentation unnecessary, to combine freedom with the pro-tective atmosphere of a home, that I felt happy. The disad-vantages of existence were mainly physical discomfort: constant gnawing hunger, the misery of a basement lavatory which on early winter mornings was damp and cold from air that came through the black iron railings of the basement area in a miasma of white fog which seeped into the damp squares of old newspaper that had to do for toilet paper; a frightening place after dark, so that after bedtime I would plead to be allowed to use the one indoor lavatory, reserved for adults, and think myself privileged when Zoë said yes.

Although the basement lavatory was not a very inviting place on a cold foggy morning, it was also a private hiding place, a retreat from the world where I would bolt myself in when I wanted to get away from everybody and everything. After all, it was community life of sorts, and the lavatory was the one place where I could brood undisturbed, let the mask slip. By now I had begun to understand that my life involved playing a role, in the dormitory, in the classroom, even at play. It was necessary to appear happy, cheerful and integrated within the group, and in a situation where one was eating, sleeping, working and playing together it was necessary to find a bolt hole in order to give way to one's inner feelings.

The lavatory was an odd place to choose, but it had the advantage of not being odd, to all outward appearances. One was simply doing the normal thing, and the only danger was in being in there too long, suspiciously so. Occasionally someone would try the latch, or kick at the wooden slats of the door. I held my breath, anxious in case a small freckled face tried to peer under the door, since there was a six-inch gap between the bottom and the stone floor. I kept very quiet, made sure my feet were out of the line of vision. Breathed out when the footsteps went away.

Before the war, when we owned a weekend house on the wooded outskirts of Berlin with its lakes and rivers, I would hide under a currant bush in the garden to brood. If the call came for lunch I would stay put, wanting someone to come and find me. Now I did not want to be found, but to come out of my own accord when I was good and ready. I needed time to work through my miseries, loneliness, even homesickness. Most often I thought of my grandmother, now so far away, unreachable in far-off Germany, who used to be the one to comfort and spoil me.

92

Locked in the lavatory, the biggest threat to my secret was Isolde. She was the one most likely to get suspicious, to ruthlessly nose and pry until she had exposed my odd behaviour. We were sparring partners, she and I. We could not leave each other alone, we were drawn to each other by a mutual respect for each other's intelligence which made us necessary companions, inevitable friends, but Isolde had an attacking streak in her make-up which could be almost vindictive: she could not stand softness, sentiment or weakness. If she sensed a vulnerable area in someone, particularly me, she would pitch in and draw blood. Volatile, critical, filled with a nervous energy which no amount of activity could quite use up, she scorned anything which smacked of emotion or introverted behaviour. She was tough and unsympathetic to her younger sister, who was quiet and subdued, obviously unhappy and homesick. She would come to Isolde for comfort and get sent packing with a flea in her ear. No doubt it was a defence mechanism on Isolde's part. She was holding her own by playing the warrior, the nervous redhead who always had to be in control, both of herself and other people.

So I was afraid of Isolde. If she once found out that I was locking myself in the lavatory to *think*, she would tell all the younger children about my odd behaviour, and they were like putty in her hands.

I had made the decision that I wanted to write, and to my surprise Isolde did not scoff at my efforts. Once I had written a story she would read it almost respectfully, with quiet interest, amused and a bit intrigued at my curious hobby. Although she was a voracious reader the notion of starting to write for oneself as another form of entertainment, at least as absorbing, if not more so, had not occurred to her, and if she thought me slightly mad to try, she respected my ambition and read those first clumsy efforts with great seriousness.

I wrote poems too, in a small black notebook which rapidly filled up with rhymes about nature and the changing seasons, but I kept these efforts to myself. I knew I was still light years away from the dream of being a writer, which had come to me one dreary wintry afternoon, walking the last yards of Lewis

Lane to turn into the creaking iron gate, past the privet hedge and the stone gatepost: a vision of years spent collecting all the wonderful words in the world in a huge thick book of blank white pages.

* * *

The town was full of soldiers. Coming to the gates of Cirencester Park on our afternoon walks we would pass the Armoury, built for the old militia in the last century to look like a sham fortified castle but abandoned for lack of wars. At long last it had come into its own, and rows of army lorries stood parked outside. On most days several soldiers would be lounging about, bored, waiting. They would laugh and wave at us, a small group of children marching two by two.

There was a time when any khaki figure seen in the distance might, with luck, turn round and become my father. But not now, since his unit had been posted to another town. So the soldiers outside the park gates were only interesting in that they were a bit like my father, and one could always indulge in hope at the sight of a khaki uniform, however remote, or be reminded. But the lorries continued to fascinate me each time we passed them. They had painted discs which were supposed to change colour if there was poison gas in the air, and I looked at them each time with a mixture of curiosity and alarm. Life was odd: here nobody bothered to carry a gasmask, and once in the park we would be miles away from home.

We marched through the gates into the park and broke ranks. Zoë occasionally brought some of her large store of ship's biscuits, and would give one to each of us halfway through a cold, hungry afternoon, as we shuffled our way through layers of damp old leaves, only to find that the last beechnuts below had all mouldered. The thick round biscuits were large and tasteless, but had the advantage of being so hard that it was almost impossible to bite into them, even at the risk of breaking one's teeth. As a result, we could make them last the whole afternoon, and enjoy the illusion of satisfying our hunger. I suppose they came from the bottom of some old store cupboard, though God knows how they got there, presumably years before the war. But

Zoë's reference to them as the hard tack of seamen, tough men tossing about on the rough seas for months, sleeping in hammocks and living rough, gave them a certain glamour, made us feel that, gnawing our way through them with so much difficulty, we somehow shared in their hardships, had become tough, like them, could almost taste salt tang and feel the waves tossing. Spiritually, in trying to eat the stuff, we had joined up and become part of the war effort.

* * *

The Armoury on Cecily Hill was too small for a world war. In 1939 the War Office had a tendency to requisition in haste and repent at leisure. In September 1939 requisitioning, like evacuation, tended to be wholesale, over-hasty, and—in the event—unnecessary. The day war broke out the Bingham Library in Dyer Street was closed, and the librarian given just twenty-four hours to move his stock. Having temporarily shifted all the books to a nearby hotel, new premises were then found only a few yards from the original library, which stood empty for a year before a use was found for it as a service canteen. And yet the demand for books, for reading material of any kind, was to be higher than ever before.

The Corn Hall in the Market Place, also requisitioned, was given back to the town after about a year and went back to its pre-war function of providing a centre for dances and entertainment, except that now the demand for amusement, as for books, was much higher, and the hall was packed out with service men and local girls on a Saturday night. The wartime mania for dancing was already in full swing.

Life speeded up in the sleepy market town. The two local cinemas received a licence to show films on Sundays. A mobile canteen appeared in the Market Place, and Brigadier Brian Horrocks of the Infantry Brigade, in temporary occupation of the Bingham Hall before the Pioneer Corps moved in, tried to speed things up even further by proposing a one-way traffic system through the narrow streets. The scheme was adopted by the council, but old ways die hard, and a year later locals were still being prosecuted for failing to adapt to the change.

The population increased almost overnight. Whole firms evacuated from the cities, as well as children, families, soldiers and airmen. And the military build-up continued. By 1944 there were more than a few lorries parked outside the Armoury: from February of that year the whole of the huge park was closed to the public, a security area. Under the old trees, through acre upon acre of parkland, thousands of military vehicles stood waiting for D-Day.

★   ★   ★

The bookshop is still there, in the Market Place, bearing the same name that was rubber-stamped in blue into the fly-leaf of my childhood Bible. My name was on the fly-leaf too: I had tried to rub it out later, but the heavily pressed pencil still leaves the clumsy lettering clearly legible—Eva Unger, Leigh Heath School, Arkenside, Lewis Lane, Cirencester. Superimposed in ink now, the letters joined up, except for unattached capitals, I later wrote merely my name and the date: April 15th, 1941. My expectation of permanence had proved false.

The bookshop in the Market Place looked much the same, still redolent of old wood shelves and floor as on the morning of my ninth birthday. But the stock is very different now: newspapers, magazines, tourist guides, illustrated popular books. The woman behind the high counter looked as though she should have belonged to the days when it was quiet and dark, with few customers, an occasional browser, and the shelves behind her head stocked with real books. Instead there was a constant flow of customers wanting small items sold in any newsagent's shop, and she coped with crisp politeness.

Banks, newspaper offices, most of the main shops still stood where I remembered them, retained their old names, although the stock had changed a little over the years. The large oldfashioned chemist near the church where Zoë had bought a mysterious preparation called Bemax, which she sprinkled on food for purposes which were not clear to me, except that they were 'good' for one; where my mother, before her departure, had bought tins of Glucodin, powdery white glucose which we sprinkled on our food because sugar was scarce, and was occasionally rammed down our throats by the spoonful in a way which was pleasant but liable to make one choke with tickly dust, to prevent us collapsing on our growing feet for lack of energy.

The large glass jars of cod liver oil and malt were also purchased here, and once a day we lined up in the scullery to have a black sticky spoonful pushed into our grimacing mouths. Cod liver oil and malt was as much a fact of everyday life for wartime children as call-up papers were for adults. Responsible adults were united in the belief that children would succumb to the first coughs and colds of winter, because of an inadequate diet, if they were not subjected to a daily, nauseating dose of fish extract, and messy, glutinous cod liver oil and malt was the usual and most popular medication. Hillie had no compunction about using the same spoon for the entire school, just as she scrubbed us all in a communal bath. Later in the war capsules of halibut liver oil became popular: they were easy enough to swallow, but invariably regurgitated a very nasty taste moments later.

Children were purged as well as fortified, because for some reason constipation was regarded as highly dangerous. At a very early age it had been drummed into me that failure to perform properly once a day would mean my insides getting blocked up and finally bursting, with fatal results, and I was sufficiently awestruck by this terrible prospect to tell the truth. Castor oil was the usual remedy, and nasty enough to seem like the sword of Damocles.

Primed with oil, purged with oil, small children were never left alone. The first sign of a cough or cold, and preparations like Vick were vigorously rubbed into the chest. Vests and liberty bodices became permanently impregnated with their odour. An innocent boil meant a series of hot kaolin poultices, producing painful scalds on the skin. As for running a temperature, that was never allowed to take its natural course. The received doctrine was that a temperature had to be sweated out, and my most tormented memories of childhood illness are of being made to stay in bed, stacked round with hot water bottles, with at least six blankets and an eiderdown piled on top of me. Hot, miserable, unable to move, I thought the hours would never pass.

Later I suffered, being liable to bronchitis most winters, but in Cirencester I seem to have been remarkably hardy, apart from chilblains, given our spartan living conditions. It was my brother, once a fat baby, always fond of his food, who now looked pale and miserable, until I could not bear the mute accusation in his eyes when he looked at me, his older sister, who should have offered some sort of help but could do nothing, had no clue what to do. A course of ultra-violet treatment did him no good, though it seems to have been regarded as a popular cure-all. In March 1941 the local Memorial Hospital, founded in memory of a Bathurst wife, reported that during the year just ended 222 patients had been admitted, 273 X-rays had been done, and 2,162 'massage and U.V. light treatments were given'.

*　*　*

The Memorial Hospital, on the outskirts of town near the old Museum and opposite the railway station, still functioned on a subscription basis when war broke out, and had financial difficulties as a result. It, too, was promptly evacuated on September 1st 1939, and the admission of patients was restricted for several weeks. To add to its difficulties, there was a fall in revenue because many contributors joined the forces, but it managed to carry on, helped by charitable handouts which were regularly acknowledged by the matron in the local newspaper each week: a dozen eggs from Lady Bathurst, fruit and vegetables from various donors, silver paper collected by a local school, a bundle of old magazines. It was a continuation of an old tradition which had kept the ladies of the town graciously occupied for generations, with a Lady Bathurst usually in the van. In January 1903 Countess Bathurst presided over a meeting of the. Primrose League at Cirencester House. The proceeds of the comic opera *Eva and the Moon-men*, it was decided, should be divided in proportions of two-thirds to one-third between Cirencester Cottage Hospital and Fairford Cottage Hospital. Unfortunately the expenses of the theatrical production had been very heavy, and there was only £12 17s to hand over. In the same week Harry Fielding, aged 34, a tramp of 6 ft 2¼ in, and Daniel Armstrong, aged 38, also a tramp, were both committed to 21 days' hard labour for refusing to break stones at the Cirencester Workhouse. The Board of Guardians were much concerned with the problem of the unworthy poor, the large number of vagrants who turned up at the workhouse each week, and later in the same year they discussed a scheme to send tramps to labour colonies for a period of three years, to be taught to work, and turned into respectable members of society. The scheme was eventually dropped as idealistic but unworkable.

In 1940 the tradition of charity for the worthy poor was as alive as ever. It had been taken over by the landed gentry when they took over the property of the Augustine monks, who once cared for the old and sick, and whose ancient hospital of St. John, a shell of stone arches, still stands. In August 1940 the following advertisement appeared on the front page of the local newspaper for several successive issues:

ST. JOHN'S HOSPITAL AND OTHER ALMSHOUSE CHARITIES, CIRENCESTER.

The Trustees of these Charities GIVE NOTICE as follows:

(1) That they are about to elect an Almsperson to the vacant Almshouse in the Whiteway.

(2) Poor Widows or Spinsters of good character, of not less than 50 years of age, who have been resident in the Parish of Cirencester for not less than 5 years next preceding the time of their appointment, who are not at the time of their appointment in receipt of Poor-law relief other than medical relief, and who from age, ill-health, accident or infirmity, are unable to maintain themselves by their own exertions, are eligible for the appointment.

Preference will be given to those who have shown reasonable providence, and to those who have been longest resident in the Parish.'

Even today the town bears evidence in stone of a long tradition of charity doled out by the ruling caste, benevolent paternalism and a Poor Law somewhat less than benevolent. The old

99

workhouse stands, an empty stone shell, after being used for years as a geriatric hospital. Backing on to its overgrown grounds, a wilderness of weeds and nettles, the Bowlby alms-houses, a neat row of terraced houses with mullioned windows and roses in the garden trellised along the covered walk. Nearby a small graveyard, closed now, the stones drowned in weeds.

Bowlby was very unlike the patrician Bathursts. He built a Temperance Hall in a town renowned for its numerous inns. In 1852 he unsuccessfully offered himself as a parliamentary candidate for nomination by anyone who advocated parliamentary reform, the ballot, free trade etc. A forlorn banner, bound to go unheeded in a rotten pocket borough where a few families ruled and one man was king.

The war gave a new impetus to good works. Ladies sat on committees, organised the evacuee hospital which was set up above a shop in Cricklade Street and collected cots and blankets and toys. Reception committees made tea and sandwiches for new arrivals from London, collected old clothes for the slum children who had suddenly landed in their midst, or helped run service canteens or the canteen for evacuees and visiting mothers. Collections and appeals—clothes for children who had arrived without a change of underwear, old pianos to entertain the troops, books and magazines for men at sea. The *Standard* ran an appeal for reading matter for the men on destroyers, motor torpedo boats and mine-sweepers. 'They like a thriller, of course, but they are not averse to what we call "more serious" books. They are fond of the Victorians and they are fond of Thackeray and Dickens, and—believe it or not—of poetry.'

No book or magazine was ever thrown away during the war. No matter how old or tattered, how outdated or stupid the contents might seem, sooner or later someone would arrive with a sack to collect the pile. I could never imagine soldiers or sailors browsing in bunk or hammock over the tripe I was prepared to give away. In fact much of the reading matter ended up as waste paper, collected with as much seriousness as metal and bones.

We had our own charity at Arkenside, prompted by Zoë and Hillie: Dr. Barnardo's Homes. Every Saturday the pay book came out and each child received sixpence. The collection box stood at the corner of the table, ready for our contribution the moment our pocket money had been handed out, our names ticked off in the exercise book. Any lingering reluctance to part with our money had been undermined by the Dickensian horror and pathos attached to the orphanage and its founder's name. We had been regaled, one wintry afternoon, with the sad story of how Dr. Barnardo had found and sheltered his first ragged, shivering, and starved orphans. In our minds he moved with missionary zeal through a dark jungle of back alleys and dirty streets which existed, not in faraway Africa, the dark territory of Livingstone, but in our midst, a strange and mysterious fact which duly appalled us. We felt very lucky. We were made to feel responsible, and genuinely wanted to give what we could.

All war children were inculcated at an early age with the idea of doing their bit for charity and for the war effort. We collected silver paper with great enthusiasm. Sunday schools were still prompting children to part with money for 'our missionaries' converting little black children to Christianity in Africa; back in London, I still put pennies in a *pâpier-maché* cottage, for Dr. Barnardo; I also found myself embroiled in a scheme whereby my friends were allowed to stick stamps, to complete a picture, on a card at so much a time to complete a picture and support the Royal Free Hospital.

Cirencester, a close-knit community where everybody knew everybody else, and with a long tradition of charitable good works organised by the local ruling caste, was admirably adapted to collect money, silver paper, old clothes, and to run soup kitchens. Scarcely a week went by without some function being organised in aid of some war fund or charity. Razor blades were collected in the Market Place, knitting wool in the cinema. No doubt prompted by the lack of petrol, a local lady sold her Rolls-Royce and gave the proceeds (£80) to help make up the deficit of the Memorial Hospital. A schoolboys' 'sing-song' at the Corn Hall after the harvest raised £2 10s for the Red Cross: the boys had been taking part in the Public Schoolboys'

Harvesting Camps in the area. Local farmers organised a sale of sheep and cattle at the Cattle Market in aid of the Red Cross and raised about £3,000, though the livestock was not the only attraction: a series of stalls were set up along one side of the Tetbury Road and a bearskin rug, a brass fender, a 'Permanent Wave' from Clappens, and a carved oak chair 'made by a Belgian Refugee in the last War' were advertised among the attractions for sale. Lord Bathurst acted as auctioneer for a while, and not only sold a box of cigars several times over, but raised £1 15s on an onion which had been sent from Canada 'in view of the supposed shortage of this vegetable in this country'.

A good time was had by all on these occasions. People called out of retirement or semi-retirement to 'do their bit' found themselves busier and happier than for a long time. Daisy Bracher, dashing round the town in a matron's uniform between the evacuee children's sick bay in Cricklade Street, the adult sick bay in Quern's Lane, the home for bedwetting children in Cecily Hill, and the home for incontinent old people who could not be billeted with private families. The childless woman who became a W.V.S. organiser and took in four children, who are remembered with tears of nostalgic joy. The rather lonely shopkeeper with an inherited business in the town, a soldier in the First World War, who had helped teach youngsters to fly in the Air Training Corps, with a group at Fairford and another at Lechlade.

But there was more than a touch of the missionary about these good folk, set in their ways, good Christians all. They found the horde of evacuees touching but dirty, in need of clean socks and instant de-lousing, and above all, little heathens in need of Christian teaching. There were also murmurs about the unworthy poor: complaints raised in council meetings about 'well-to-do' people who refused to pay their own way by claiming the 5s billeting allowance for evacuees who came from a danger area. Nearly forty years on the Town Clerk of the time, who was also the Billeting Officer, recalls with regret that the people who abused the system by claiming their grant from the Post Office were mostly Jews, and he had even seen one of them wearing a fur coat. In September 1941 the Cirencester Rural District Council had considered the case of an elderly couple with a joint income of £315 a year, who had declined to make a contribution to the cost of the billeting allowance. The income seems modest enough, even by the standards of 1941, but perhaps the couple was Jewish and she wore a fur coat of sorts. The ex-town clerk has not forgotten those Jews, though it pained him to name the culprits by race, nor has he forgiven them. On the other hand, he told me, quite a few evacuees stayed on after the war, and 'many have made good'.

11

WHEN WILLIAM STUKELEY came to Cirencester early in the eighteenth century he visited Mr. Isaac Tibbot of Castle Street, who had in his possession the gravestone of a Roman woman, Julia Casta. It was one of five tombstones found in a row 'upon the north side of the Foss road, called *Quern* from the quarries of stone thereabouts'. Mr. Tibbot used another of the tombstones as a garden table, whilst a third made a convenient footbridge across a ditch in Castle Street. It seems that Mr. Tibbot had also acquired some of the bones: 'He keeps Julia Casta's skull in his summer-house; but people have stole all her teeth out for amulets against the ague.'

When it comes to pain, human superstition does not change very much: in retrospect their efforts all seem pathetic and futile. Evidence of Roman attempts to cope with disease were found in the shape of seals and stamps unearthed in the Leauses. A hundred years after Stukeley came to Cirencester the local newspaper, founded in 1837, was urging its readers to buy Woodhouse's Balsam of Spermaceti as a cure for coughs, Frank's Specific Solution of Copaiba and Wray's Balsamic Pills for kidney and bladder complaints and 'seminal weakness'; Dinneford's Indian Tonic was recommended for weak stomachs, and Dr. Bayfield's Spasmodic Tincture was recommended 'To Female Invalids'—'No less than 31,000 FEMALES have expired from diseases peculiar to their sex, in one year . . . See the Registrar-General's Report', warned the advertisement.

That was in 1841. In 1941 people's ailments, and certainly their fears, had changed remarkably little. The *Standard* still sold about the same proportion of its advertising space to the promoters of patent medicines: Doans for 'Lazy Kidneys', and

Carter's Little Liver Pills. And the female constitution was still considered remarkably vulnerable: if they did not go so far as to expire, they certainly wilted. Dr. Williams' Pink Pills were recommended both for 'women suffering the critical years of middle age' and for girls in their early teens who were causing their mothers anxiety by 'dull eyes, pallid cheeks, a languid step, fits of depression, an aching back, periodical headaches, and a dislike of proper food'. The advertisement claimed that 'Thousands of unhappy, feeble, anaemic girls have been transformed into robust women through the good red blood these pills infust into the system.'

Another problem for the mothers of growing girls was, apparently, bowels. 'That is why doctors and nurses recommend a regular liquid laxative. But any strong medicine may easily harm the child and lead to serious internal troubles in later life. The ideal liquid laxative for the female constitution is "California Syrup of Figs" because it is efficient yet gentle and safe. Give your daughters a dose once a week to make sure that the bowels are clean and entirely free from poisonous waste.'

In an age of much self-medication, advertisers tried to exploit the increased anxiety of mothers as food became scarce. California Syrup of Figs was soon advertised as a defence against colds and by the autumn of 1940 even Oxo and Ovaltine were supposed to help children resist the onslaught of winter coughs and colds. But the copywriters found their exploitation of the traditionally frail female constitution increasingly difficult to maintain in the face of wartime reality. Aspro regularly took large spaces in the *Standard*, and at first aimed its copy at 'women who suffered with their nerves more than previous generations'. But by the summer of 1941 they had changed their tune: 'For women answering the nation's call—the women of Britain are responding nobly to the nation's call. In the services—in field or factory—in the home—they show their courage and initiative. The modern woman's endurance is often amazing! Nevertheless, the strenuousness of it all sometimes threatens to become overwhelming.'

In fact, many women took to smoking. And perhaps they found the brewery advertisements more appealing: 'In this

War of Nerves you'll find Stroud Beer a Pillar of Strength'. Unfortunately the beer ran out, and brewers first had to appeal to the public to drink less rather than more, and finally donated their advertising space to the nation for a series of 'What do I do?' notices designed to instruct the public: 'What do I do . . . when I hear guns, explosions, air-raid warnings? I keep a cool head. I take cover. I gather my family with gasmasks, and go quietly to my shelter or refuge room. I do *not* try to "have a look." I do *not* rush about alarming people. I remember that a lot of noise is a *good* noise—our guns firing at the enemy. And I remember the odds are thousands to one against my being hurt. Cut this out—and keep it!' And even more alarming: 'What do I do if I hear news that Germans are trying to land or have landed? I do *not* get panicky. I *stay put*. I say to myself: "Our chaps will deal with them." I do *not* say, "I must get out of here." I remember that fighting men must have clear roads. I do *not* go on to the road on bicycle, in car or on foot.'

Cirencester had no air raids to worry about, and the two sirens in the town were anyhow inaudible to a large proportion of the population, but possible invasion was a matter for concern. Various cycling clubs wrote to the *Standard* about ways in which bicycles could be immobilised in case of invasion, so that they would not be useful to the enemy. Owners of bicycles were advised to remove the pedals, or the nuts of the back wheel, 'hiding in all cases the parts involved'. It was even suggested that pedals should be removed immediately, without waiting for an invasion warning. How the owners were supposed to get to and from work before this invasion of Germans, apparently equipped with little more than bicycle clips, was not made clear.

The farmer's wife whom I watched churning butter with such muscular vigour might have laughed, but the conventional image of woman was taking hard knocks owing to the exigencies of war. Perhaps the gentlemen who sat on committees had managed to turn an unseeing eye, all their lives, on the hard lot of the working woman before the war, when she scrubbed his floor after he left for the office. In May 1941 the Gloucestershire

Highways Committee decided that women should be employed on roads to release men for other work. 'Mr. J. Matthews asked whether it was intended that the women should clean ditches out, do hedging, and things like that. The County Surveyor, Mr. E. C. Boyce, replied that it was so. Mr. Matthews rejoined: "Surely we have not come to that?" The Chairman, Captain R. A. Bennett, observed: "It looks as though we are coming to it." ' The gentlemen decided that if we had indeed come to such a pass the women should at least get a reasonable wage, but the proposal to pay them a shilling an hour was defeated after it had been pointed out that women land workers were being employed for a mere 8d an hour, which would cause too much of a discrepancy. Having digested this new and somewhat embarrassing insight into the lives of working women the gentlemen of the committee decided to employ the women at 10d an hour. Four months later it was reported that forty-five women were now employed on roadwork in the county, and that 'the women had satisfactorily undertaken the light duties, such as white line painting'. No doubt the usual male face-saving adjustment had taken place in the interim, whereby any work undertaken by women is automatically described as 'light'. In the same month the minimum agricultural wage for men was raised from 48s to 52s per week, but the minimum wage for women workers remained unchanged at 36s per week.

Apart from the demands of voluntary work and the constant nuisance of evacuees in the spare bedroom the housewives of Cirencester had an easy war compared to women in the big cities. With gardens, and farms in the neighbourhood, the realities of food rationing were not as harsh as elsewhere. Zoë was not the only person to become an enthusiastic beekeeper, and a local shop which specialised in the necessary equipment did good business. The outmoded fashion of cottagers' pigs was revived, and although the Cirencester Rural District Council Food Control Committee asked people who slaughtered a pig to cancel the appropriate coupons in their ration books, it is difficult to imagine that this requirement did not go by default, more often than not. A Pig Club was started in the town, and the pigs in the communal piggery were fed from waste collected by the W.V.S. Although 'pig bins' for waste food were a common enough feature of life in London, public spirited people in Cirencester could invest between 10s and £2 in the Pig Club and get bacon in return for their waste. And there was a special sugar allowance for people who grew enough fruit to make their own jam.

In spite of this in-built advantage when it came to food rationing, the Cirencester housewife's food consciousness had to be raised, and a barrage of propaganda came her way. The Ministry of Food constantly published household hints to help the war effort. In September 1941, to coincide with a bumper blackberry season, the Ministry published a recipe for blackberry jam, together with tips on how to make grated carrot sandwiches, rusks from stale bread, and advice on cooking the green bits of cauliflowers. 'Use the remains of today's rice pudding to thicken to-morrow's soup' and 'Eat more plums. Plums are in season now', together with a recipe for potato carrot pancakes—such titbits were regularly aimed at women readers, alternating with admonitions from the Mines Department to 'Go Easy with the Poker' and official notices like REGISTER NOW FOR MEAT. Other organisations did their bit to re-educate the housewife. The local Women's Institute organised a lecture on fruit bottling during the soft fruit season, and the Cirencester Gas Company held a series of cookery demonstrations at the Congregational School Room on jam-making, fruit bottling, and the making of chutney and pickles. And for a population rapidly getting tired of fish and tapioca a cookery book entitled *What Famous People Eat in Wartime* helped to encourage the notion that we were all in this together. Mr. Chamberlain, it seemed, liked a homely fish and leek pie, Lady Halifax favoured savoury haddock, and the Postmaster General, Member of Parliament for Cirencester, also shared a partiality for haddock, creamed.

In retrospect I feel rather guilty at the way we giggled at the solemn Cirencester waitress with her daily glum chant of 'Rice pudding and stewed pears'. She should have reminded us that there was a war going on. My mother was to remind us often enough, in the years to come, as we sighed and complained and poked dispiritedly at the third supper of fish in a week, but in the golden autumn of 1940 we regarded the small town of Cirencester and its environs as a place rich in the good things of life. Preston's, the grocer in Cricklade Street, had shelves crammed with jars of jam and other goodies, the ground floor of Viner's near the Market Place had glass shelves stocked with mouth-watering buns and cream cakes, and the surrounding countryside had treasures of its own: berries in the hedgerows, cows trudging back to the sheds at dusk, their udders heavy with milk; warm eggs to be found in the henhouse; and cream turned to butter in the trundling churn in the dairy across the yard from the farmhouse kitchen which always had a comfortable smell of food, of hams smoking from the ceiling and pie pastry turning brown in the huge oven.

* * *

Apart from collecting money for the war a good deal of local thought and energy went into the problem of collecting scrap. In 1940 the Council set up a special committee for the salvage of waste, and arranged for the ever-ready W.V.S. to make house-to-house calls. The public was instructed to keep waste paper and bones in separate bundles. 'With the present meat ration most of us will not have many bones, but we need them all.'

The results were unexpectedly gratifying. Within a month the Cirencester Urban District Council announced that 200 pounds of bones were now being collected each week. As for metal, exclusive of old guns, six or seven tons of miscellaneous metal had accumulated, and more was still coming in. However, the public was reminded not to get complacent or slack in their efforts. In the words of Herbert Morrison, Minister of Supply: 'Every piece of paper, every old bone, every piece of scrap metal is a potential bullet against Hitler. We would never fling away a bullet. We must never fling away one piece of scrap which can be salvaged.'

The Government did not regard Cirencester as a vulnerable area, and no provisions were made for air raid shelters in private homes, but the Urban District Council decided to kill two birds with one stone by issuing householders with leaflets which required them to clear their attics to reduce the fire risk in case of air attack, and at the same time provide valuable salvage.

A box for used razor blades was set up in the Market Place, a highly successful scheme, but the Urban District Council dragged its heels with regard to the Ministry of Defence regulation on iron railings, gates, posts, chains, bollards and similar articles. The public was duly warned: 'Any person who claims that any iron railings, gates, posts, chains, bollards or similar articles of which they are the owner should by reason of their special artistic merit or historic interest be excluded from the survey' was required to give written notice within fourteen days. But owners need have had no fears. At a later meeting, whilst congratulating itself on the six thousand razor blades which had been collected in the Market Place, the Urban District Council postponed the matter of railings for a later meeting, a chairman's decision which obviously reflected the feelings of the meeting. Mr. Newcombe said they should not hurry in the matter at all, and that parts of Cheltenham were a disgrace to the landscape. 'It's a panic—that's all it is.'

The Council issued a notice in the local paper saying that not only railings of artistic or historic interest, but those necessary for safety reasons, or to prevent cattle straying, would also be exempted. And when the subject was again discussed at a later Council meeting the Chairman thought that the amount of railings scheduled for removal would not pay the Government to take it away. Judging from the discussion, some local inhabitants had suddenly discovered artistic merit where they had previously complained of an eyesore. One such eyesore was the nineteenth-century railing round the parish church, which stayed put until some time after the war was over.

*　　*　　*

But the grand gala, the highlight of the summer of 1941, was War Weapons Week. To me, who had no idea what the festivities were all about, it meant my introduction to a feature of Cirencester life through the centuries—the visits of Royalty.

Some of these royal arrivals had, it is true, been rather less than happy, like that of Stephen in the twelfth century who, in his fight for the succession with Matilda, daughter of Henry I who endowed the Abbey, escaped from captivity, took Cirencester by storm and razed its castle; or the visit of Charles I during the Civil War, shortly after royalist troops had captured the town. But on the whole local historians are proud of the favours bestowed on them by monarchs. Early royal patrons of the Abbey were in the habit of accepting the hospitality of the Abbot, and hunting in the extensive woodlands. Later monarchs visited their secular favourites who had taken over control of the town and its lands. Queen Elizabeth visited Cirencester in the summer of 1592 during one of her many progresses, and was presented with a gilt cup and heard an oration in Latin.

After the Restoration Charles II and Queen Anne also slept as soundly in the houses of the local gentry as Queen Elizabeth had done, and when young Allen Bathurst became a member for the borough in 1705 Her Majesty wrote to the young man's mother 'I shall always depend on his concurring in everything that is good for me and for the Publick.' Apparently she was not disappointed in her protégé. She visited young Bathurst and his wife at Oakley Grove in 1708 and three years later, when she created twelve new peers to strengthen her Tory ministry the last and youngest was Allen Bathurst, who became a Baron. The second generation, now owners of most of the surrounding land, were promoted to an earldom and could enrapture a visiting King George, Queen Charlotte and three princesses with the charm of their woods and groves.

As a foreigner I had no notion of the peculiar place which royalty occupies in English sentiment and general *Weltanschauung*, though I had been duly bewildered, on my first arrival at the London primary school, by the strange manifestations of Empire Day. Suddenly one morning, for no apparent reason other than the May sunshine, every little girl arrived with her hair festooned with red, white and blue ribbons. Some also wore pinafores in the same colour scheme, or adorned with Union Jacks. And every milk mug was a Coronation mug, shown off with pride. I did not know what the Coronation was.

It had, it seemed, taken place two years before, when I was not in the country. So I was almost alone in not owning a Coronation mug, and could not drink my school milk from it on this remarkable day of days, which had all the festive flavour I associated with the May Day of old poems and illustrated picture books.

I was conscious of something vaguely absurd, almost tribal, about this sudden mass manifestation of Union Jacks and red, white and blue ribbons blooming, not just from heads and pigtails, but any spot to which they could conveniently be tied. Who cared about the Coronation anyway, I thought, holding on to my ordinary blue and white mug, and eyeing the royal faces which looked insipid enough.

But now, in Cirencester, I was to get a taste of the real thing. I had an unexpected hors d'oeuvre a few days before the Great Day, when Zoë took me shopping with her. We were passing the church in the Market Place when I noticed a crowd of people standing around, for no apparent reason, opposite a shop on the other side of the square. Suddenly a lady in a white suit, with matching hat, handbag and shoes, emerged from a doorway. It was obvious that the bystanders had been waiting all this time to stare at her. I saw only a lady who looked like my mother on a pre-war outing, slim, high-heeled. She stood out like a white dove amongst a crowd of drab brown birds, sparrows and thrushes, who made way for her, fluttered, moved behind her at a respectful distance as she walked slowly and sedately across the Market Place to look at the mobile canteen.

'Who', I asked Zoë, who seemed remarkably unconcerned by what was going on just across the road, and was marching at her normal brisk pace towards the chemist—'Who is that?'

'That', said Zoë, 'is the Duchess of Gloucester', as though she had known all along and took it for granted. I was puzzled that Zoë should recognise her on sight, and even more puzzled that people should stand and stare while Zoë hurried me into the chemist's shop without stopping to watch the proceedings. I concluded that since we were in Gloucestershire and the lady in white was the Duchess of Gloucester, she was normally to be seen carrying out inspections of her home grounds. Which was why Zoë knew who she was. The crowd of bystanders certainly looked as though they thought the county belonged to her in some peculiar way.

But if Zoë did not bother to stop and stare at a mere local duchess, the arrival of Queen Mary was quite another matter. There was a small shop at the corner of the Market Place, near the church but apart from it, the only one to the left of the church on the north side of the Market Place, and the only one with a low flat roof. Arrangements had been made with the shopkeeper, and on this momentous afternoon the whole school, children and staff, were escorted up the narrow staircase to a unique vantage point. Just below us was the especially erected stand, facing us and the church, where Her Majesty would be received.

We watched the scene from the low rooftop, which conveniently had a parapet just the right height for small children. The Market Place had been transformed: it fluttered with bunting and flags, and the space round the royal stand was bright with uniforms and musical instruments. Shopkeepers had draped their frontages with flags, strings of coloured pennants were strung from the central stand across the Market Place, and baskets of flowers dangled from the top of lampposts. The Home Guard were lined up, so were a contingent of sailors, and the Royal Air Force Band gave a rendering of the National Anthem as the black car, escorted by motor cycles, drove slowly into the Market Place from the direction of Cirencester House.

There was no doubt about this one: she was something special, with the regal severity of her expression, unsmiling, the toque on her head, the long straight coat almost to her ankles. She moved as though she had a poker down her back, and was escorted by tubby Earl Bathurst and his wife, with whom she had just taken tea, up the steps of the covered stand.

A loudspeaker system had been rigged up, and a gentleman made a speech into it, which was almost impossible to understand. He was, anyhow, the right honourable representative at Westminster, very boring and of no interest. His words reverberated round the square, garbled and hollowed by the speaker

E   113

system. What were interesting were the soldiers and the band and austere figure of the Queen Mother. What was most interesting of all, for the pupils of Leigh Heath School, peering down from the roof, was the figure of the small girl in pink who walked up the steps of the dais, made a curtsey, and handed Her Majesty a bouquet of flowers almost as large as herself. Not a heart, leaning against the low parapet, but did not beat with something approaching envy. Shirley Temple herself was put in the shade.

The boring men on the platform stopped talking and Queen Mary, having descended the steps with a minimum of assistance from the plump earl, who kept circling round her making anxious gestures of solicitude, did not return to the waiting car. Instead she marched quite alone through the north porch and disappeared into the church. She did not come out again. The proceedings hung in abeyance and began, finally, to disintegrate. It seemed that the troops and the band were being instructed by their officers to pack up and call it a day. The crowds lining the pavement began to thin and drift away. I was intrigued by her solitary, ramrod walk into the church. She was paying one more social call, a very private one. I thought she had gone in there to talk rather than pray, that in leaving behind the ordinary people gathered in the Market Place, she had sought refuge in the house of the one person who was her equal in rank: God. And having found a kindred spirit with whom she could discuss matters of state, of high moment, she simply refused to come back out.

We were led back down the narrow staircase through the shop, to the pavement, still crowded with people, some standing aimlessly about, others walking off home under the flags and bunting.

*　*　*

My view of royalty was somewhat simplified, though not necessarily false. It was whispered that Queen Mary was staying in the neighbourhood, and that as a royal evacuee she had graciously condescended to pay the town a visit seemed explanation enough. No wonder there was so much fuss: unlike the Duchess of Gloucester, it would never have been her stomping ground in normal peacetime.

In fact the Duchess had been doing her patriotic duty by inspecting a Red Cross supply depot, and Queen Mary had come to launch War Weapons Week, the town's most ambitious contribution to the war effort to date. None of this penetrated my child's skull. Perhaps the loudspeaker system was at fault. Maybe I was simply beguiled by the flowers and bunting, the red carpet and the little girl with the bouquet, into thinking we were celebrating a royal visit, rather than helping to fight the war. That was going on elsewhere, back home in London, without bands or bunting, only people scampering for shelter as the siren wailed for the third or fourth time in a day. Rubble, drab streets, brick air raid shelters, sandbags; heavy Anderson shelters in small front living rooms, static water tanks going green and scummy at the corner of the street, rows of bunks in the underground. That was war. This sunny June afternoon was a festival.

The declared objective of War Weapons Week, the highlight of the 1941 summer season, was to sell War Bonds, and the target of £100,000 might have been thought over-ambitious after the abortive Spitfire Fund of the previous year, except that with War Bonds the buyers had some expectation of getting their money back. In fact the public got their money's worth in other ways, including an almost non-stop street theatre acting out the war in miniature. This was fun for the native inhabitants of Cirencester, who had not had occasion to see much of the real war at first hand.

Sunday, the day after the royal visit, being the Lord's day, was given over to open-air services in the Market Place, and the various denominations, high and low, united in prayer and choir singing, accompanied by a local band. But on Monday things began to hot up. At eight o'clock in the evening when, owing to British Double Summer Time, it was still broad daylight and the show was clearly visible to spectators, 'enemy' bombers swooped over the town. Three explosions were timed to go off and the King's Head having been declared hit, its inmates were promptly rescued. The dramatic air raid was immediately followed by a gas alert. A small gas bomb had landed outside Barclay's Bank, by prior arrangement. Wardens cautiously approached the lethal object, unrecognisable to their friends in a weird assortment of gasmasks, curtains, gas-proof clothing and gumboots. Having recognised the signs of mustard gas, they sounded the gas rattle, and two men were treated for liquid gas on their skins with bleach paste from a bucket duly placed in the doorway of the nearby Boots, since it was planned that all chemists would have such a bucket in their doorways once gas attacks started. Forewarned is fore-armed; the exercise ran according to plan, and the local inhabitants got a preview of what, in the event, never happened.

Wednesday evening was a big night. Half the town turned out, and four thousand people stood agog to watch a fire-fighting display in the Market Place. The hosepipes were direc-ted at the tower of the church and, according to the local reporter on the *Standard*, the display was 'not without its humorous element'. 'Smoke was seen to ensue from the window of the top storey of the premises of Messrs. Hamper and Fry and a pyjama-clad figure was seen trying to reach safety.' A lady in night attire 'displaying signs of hysterical fear reactions' was also rescued: her rescuer, according to the report, provided a 'pacifier' in a dark flat bottle 'to which she attached herself with marked effect'.

The drama proceeded like a medieval miracle cycle. Every-one was either watching or taking part. On Thursday evening big bombers flew over the town. Nobody ran for cover. Instead, thousands of enthralled spectators stood staring up at the sky as the planes were engaged in combat by Hurricanes and other fighter planes from nearby airfields. For over an hour the pilots gave a breathtaking display of aerobatics, twisting and turning and looping the loop, and diving to the attack. Then they all went home and the spectators went back indoors, excited by what they had seen, the derring-do of the boys in blue. War was never like this before.

After these highlights the week finished off on a quieter note. Something for everyone, including the kiddies. On Friday morning there was an auction in the Market Place, and Mr.

Syd Walker, 'famous broadcasting star', disposed of miscellaneous objects, including a hive of bees. On Saturday afternoon the famous broadcasting celebrity was back on duty, giving autographs to all good children who had bought Savings Certificates or books of Saving Stamps. There was also a procession of armoured vehicles accompanied by bands through the town, starting at Cecily Hill and ending up in the Market Place after doing a round tour of the town. And the week ended up as all good festivals should, with a vaudeville show at the Corn Hall followed by a dance which spilled out into the Market Place. Syd Walker did a turn, so did a female impersonator, a 'banjovial songster from the Palladium', and Jeannette the international songbird. There was such a crush for the dance that the *Standard* laid on music from their announcement van so that the overflow could dance in the Market Place. Nothing like it was to be seen again until VE Day. In fact, one might have thought the war was already won.

* * *

It was a fun war, that week. Moreover, £365,152 was raised in War Bonds, nearly four times the original target. Of course somebody had to sound a sour note. A correspondent complained to the local paper that smoke had continued to billow from the local flour mill in a very disloyal manner during the royal visit. The manager replied that, far from being disloyal, they were obeying the injunctions of the Ministry of Food. Some people, it seemed, really had forgotten the purpose of the visit. They still could not get it into their heads that there was a war going on.

12

QUEEN MARY's visit came in the high summer of 1941, when the restrictions of the schoolroom seemed at their lowest. The garden was flowering and lime-scented, and the swing was in constant use. Instead of an indoor performance of the Mad Hatter's Tea Party, a few parents and selected guests who happened to be in the district were regaled with a dramatic recitation of *Hiawatha* on the lawn, which had enough of a slope to provide the illusion of a stage. Isolde had star billing on this occasion, striding about somewhat melodramatically in sandals and short cotton frock, while I stood meekly in the background being a chorus. The compelling rhythm had an obvious appeal for Isolde, who spoke with gusto, moving with long, jerky strides to make full use of all the grass space between gravel path and flower border. Nobody else got a look in. Isolde was in command.

In the park the buttercups came high above our waists in grass which was left uncut that summer. We dipped in it, moved and sank and rolled as though it had been a green sea in which we could bathe, put the lacquered yellow cups under our chins and found out that we all liked butter. On longer walks we ran rings round Pope's Seat, a small stone structure which mystified me. I kept running round the back looking for a door which, I felt, ought to have been there, as an entrance into a miniature house. The small edifice puzzled me, and I sensed a riddle, though I did not know it concerned, not a child playing houses, but a small crippled man who not only wrote poetry but helped to create my enchanted parkland, loved tall trees in contrast to his mortal puny body. 'I look upon myself as the magician appropriate to the place,' he wrote, 'without whom no mortal can penetrate into the recesses of those sacred groves.' Nobody told me about him, how he could not walk very far, needed a resting place to which he could be carried, where he could sit in solitude and versify, watching the trees grow tall, so I continued to run round the little house looking for a secret door which nobody ever found.

Unless it was in the park itself, in the massive avenue of trees which diminished man and yet represented the peak of his achievement: Nature tamed to a grand design. Standing years later in the dark and smutty atmosphere of the London Underground, waiting on a platform, the perennial old poster for Start-Rite Shoes, with two small children beginning to walk the long straight avenue of 'life', would take me straight back to the long avenue of Cirencester Park, the small boy and girl my brother and I.

The high summer days of 1941 were long, but not only childhood long. It was always daylight, and the days were interminable for another reason. We did not know about British Double Summer Time, a wartime measure to save light and electricity, we only knew that we were despatched to bed in broad daylight, and that it was quite impossible to fall asleep. We would lie awake, listening to the sounds from the next-door garden, where the dentist's children were still out at play. Occasionally one of us would creep out of bed and watch them from the window. The oldest child, a girl, had long dark hair to her waist and wore frilled pinafores. At least I think she did: the whole family merged into the story books of E. Nesbit, took over their enchanted adventures, looked like the book illustrations, played into dusk in a world of rare privilege.

It was not fair, we agreed, listening to the sounds of laughter. It was the one time we felt cooped up in an institution, in a different class, a quite separate world from the children next door. Lying in superfluous daylight, I studied the nursery posters: an illustrated alphabet starting with an apple, which I soon knew by heart, and a picture of two children, boy and girl, walking through a wood. The picture had the exaggerated illustrative quality intended for learning, with birds and a rabbit and obvious foxgloves in the foreground.

After a while the sounds of the children next door playing out in the garden would be replaced by noises from the cinema as the film swelled to a musical crescendo and the doors opened. Sometimes the film itself was a musical, and we all got heartily sick of hearing 'When you wish upon a star' because plump blonde Joyce, in the middle bed near the empty fireplace, would insist on singing the words each time, crooning to herself as she cuddled her panda pyjama case and told us about the magic of the silver screen, a world of Hollywood and glamour which had quite swallowed her up at the age of eight or nine. She was soft and silly, a marsh mallow of a child with her blonde hair and plump white body. She wore pink pyjamas and fluffy slippers and it seemed certain that, if she could not actually become a Shirley Temple or Norma Jean, she would lose herself in a lifelong daydream of celluloid and false glamour. She was impervious to the irritation she caused to the other inmates of the dormitory, particularly Isolde, as she crooned and hummed. Injunctions to 'shut up' were rapidly followed by flying pillows and the odd slipper aimed at her lost and happy head.

* * *

The times were out of joint all during the war. Clocks and sun bore little relationship to each other. The Summer Time of 1939 was extended to November and then reintroduced in February 1940 for the rest of the war. The hours of daylight at the latter end of the day were lengthened even further by Double Summer Time, which put the clocks forward a second hour from May to August in 1941, and from the beginning of April until mid-August until the war was over in 1945. Double Summer Time ended in July 1945 and British clocks went back to Greenwich Mean Time, real time, for the first time in five years in October 1945.

All this played havoc with children's bedtime. In London most of us simply went on playing in the streets, on open patches of ground, in back gardens, until the light began to fade in the summer months, or at least till eight o'clock. Most mothers had enough sense, and enough other worries, not to struggle against nature by putting their kids to bed in the middle of the afternoon. Zoë and Hillie, of course, had never been natural mothers and, just as they did not understand the ravenous appetites of small growing children, they saw nothing wrong with putting children to bed by the clock. So we lay awake for hours in the dormitory, tossing about and grumbling.

Putting the clocks forward two hours presented different problems in different areas. In London most of us spent most of the time suffering from lack of sleep. Not only were our sleeping habits being messed about by wartime clocks, when we did finally fall asleep we were, as likely as not, forced wide awake by the air raid sirens wailing through the dark. Having taken shelter and yawned through several hours of thundering anti-aircraft guns, whistling bombs, explosions, and the final high-pitched all clear, we tumbled back into bed to sleep for a couple of hours before it was time to get up and go to school.

But in country districts the problems were different. City school children and office workers might yawn their way to work in the dark, but men who worked on the land wanted daylight. Farmers protested when the scheme for Double Summer Time was first announced. At an executive meeting of the Gloucestershire Farmers' Union it was suggested that members should ignore the extra hour of Summer Time, since men on the Cotswold Hills could not be expected to start haymaking or harvesting at 5 a.m.

The Government responded to protests from rural areas by announcing that farmers would be exempted from the extra hour of Summer Time. The result was, to say the least, confusing. 'In rural districts the clocks will be put on but everything but the clock will start an hour later . . . Work on farms—now 7 a.m. till 5 p.m.—will be 8 a.m. till 6 p.m. by the clock. The schools will open at 10 a.m. instead of 9 a.m. Milk trains will run an hour later, again by the clock, and as far as possible all country services will follow suit.' The Minister of Agriculture had done his best, but was forced to admit the scheme was not foolproof. 'There may be defects where rural and urban districts overlap' he admitted, in one of the great understatements of the period.

* * *

One memorable windblown day Zoë took a group of us to nearby Stroud. We did the short journey by train and the landscape of high curved hills with their buildings like sudden cliff-faces of grey stone stayed in my memory as unique. Zoë had packed a picnic lunch, and sat perched on top of a cold windy hill handing out sandwiches as the shadows of cloud moved over the rough harassed grass and the sun came through fitfully once in a while, but not long enough to warm us up. We ran about the steep slopes to keep warm and were not sorry when it was time to seek the shelter of the valley and make for the railway station to catch the return train.

The little train wound its way through the round green hills. Impossible to imagine that countryside without its network of small railway lines, keeping the whole area alive, moving, like the nervous system in a body. In 1941, when we took that day trip to Stroud, Cirencester had been on that network for a hundred years. The Great Western Railway branch line from Swindon was opened on May 31st 1841, a fine day on which thousands of people flocked not only to the station, but to every bridge and cutting to catch their first glimpse of this new miracle of steam and iron. As always, transport innovation aroused fear and trepidation as well as excitement. A lot of people were nervous of going too near the engine, and preferred to watch the steaming monster from a safe distance, but the *Standard* was pleased to report that not a single accident happened on the opening day.

As always, Earl Bathurst was behind the new venture. In January 1838 he had presided over a meeting at the town hall, also attended by the two Members of Parliament for the borough, whose names were (surprise, surprise) Mr. Master and Mr. Cripps. The earl announced that although he had previously entertained objections to railways, he had now changed his mind, and to prove it he had ordered the purchase of some shares in the Cheltenham and Great Western Union which proposed to build the branch line. Mr. Master and Mr. Cripps also announced their intention to buy shares, Mr. Cripps having happily resolved a conflict of private interest and public duty with regard to his functions in the House of

Commons, and the meeting closed with a vote of thanks to his lordship for not standing in the way of progress: 'though objecting to the railway' he had allowed the line to cross his land. I looked forward to coming back, as I had done in the old days, sitting in a railway carriage, watching fields and grazing cattle chug past the window in a leisurely fashion. But postwar progress has been unkind to Cirencester, and the branch line was lopped off in the Beeching cuts. I felt cheated of a journey I had dreamed of for months, already travelled in my mind's eye in happy anticipation long before I was due to arrive. Coming by motorway did not count, has no more to do with making a journey and arrival than hopping on to a plane and stepping out of it an hour later. I cling to the thought that I should have come back by a slow train from Swindon: that is how I did come back, in my mind.

* * *

The disappearance of Brunel's branch line has done more than deprive me of a dream return to the past as I would have wished it to happen, has done more than disrupt a sense of continuity which otherwise belongs to this small town as the parish church has always belonged to the Market Place, the drains and subsoil to the bones of dead Romans, the town and all its works to the patronage of the earl, and the earl to his parkland. Now that both railway lines have gone for good, (and the opening of the second railway line at Watermoor in 1884 was celebrated as an immense popular event with a militia band, the explosion of detonators, a procession, triumphal arch, a public luncheon attended by the local bigwigs, and a programme of old English sports in the Market Place, with legs of mutton waiting to be won at the top of three greasy poles and a display of fireworks to round off the day), now that both railway links with the outside world have been cut the town is trapped in a stranglehold of motorways, by-passes and flyovers, like Laocoon hopelessly fighting off his snakes. The land roundabout is swallowed in asphalt and concrete. Bus services block the narrow streets, stop outside the parish church. Houses have been knocked down at the east end of the town to make way for a parking area. At the western perimeter the old railway station with its busy goods yards has become a bleak coach terminal: no bustle, no people, just an empty space and a timetable.

Curiously enough, a monument stemming from the same era as the expansion of railways still stands, derelict now, fenced off with barbed wire. Nobody knows what to do with it, a building as fine and noble in construction as its purpose was ugly. In 1836, when the Cheltenham and Great Western Union was incorporated, work also began on the construction of the workhouse with its neo-classical stone façade, not far from the proposed new railway line. The Cirencester Union, to comply with the new Poor Law, announced on August 12th 1837, in an issue of the newly established *Wiltshire and Gloucestershire Standard*, a high Tory paper dedicated to fight parliamentary reform and the erosion of privilege, that inmates of the Cirencester Workhouse would be kept alive on a diet of bread and gruel for breakfast, potatoes and soup for dinner, and bread with one ounce of cheese for supper. This was the diet for the able-bodied. 'Children under 10 years of age to be dieted at discretion; after 10 to be dieted as women.' The women were fed an ounce of bread less at breakfast and supper.

The same issue of the *Standard* was pleased to announce that, following the death of the King and the dissolution of Parliament, Messrs. Cripps and Master (Conservative) had been returned in an uncontested election.

The newly formed Guardians of the Poor were not slow to get down to business. By November 1837 they were already feeling sufficiently pleased with their efforts to give a 'sumptuous dinner' at the King's Head in honour of the Chairman, Mr. Joseph Cripps M.P., and his Vice-Chairman, a Mr. Blackwell. Eighty gentlemen sat down to dinner and although the menu was not specified, we may be sure it was more than workhouse soup and potatoes. Mr. Joseph Cripps was presented with 'a superb silver salver, value £50', the gift of the Guardians, verbosely inscribed, as 'a trifling but sincere testimony'. Mr. Cripps was reported to have made a very affecting speech, and the *Standard* added that 'The company was very much gratified, and did not separate until a late hour.' No doubt the wine had flowed freely, and the port had circulated round the table to some effect, since a proposal that 'a treat of a substantial meal should be given to the poor in the Union workhouse' was unanimously agreed to.

History does not record whether the inmates ever got such a meal. It was probably forgotten in the morning after the night before, when bonhomie gave way to headaches and dyspepsia, and the coffers could well have been seriously depleted by the previous day's expenditure. But by 1841 the Cirencester Workhouse was in bad odour far beyond the bounds of the borough. A disturbed correspondent wrote to the *Standard* that 'The London and Provincial journals tell us that five ounces of bacon on the Sunday, and watergruel or pork broth all the rest of the week, are supposed enough by the Cirencester Board of Guardians for the most deserving', and asked the Guardians of the Cirencester Union for an assurance that the report was untrue. No denial was forthcoming.

However, a week after this voice of conscience had written into the wind 'We hope that the Guardians of the Cirencester Union are in a situation to, and will assure us, that such is not the dietary of the Cirencester Union', the *Standard* was reporting, with predictable satisfaction, that William Cripps and Thomas Master had been returned unopposed. 'No other candidate being proposed, they were both declared duly elected. The members were then carried through the streets of the borough, in two handsome chairs, accompanied by the most respectable inhabitants. . . . The Electors afterwards partook of a sumptuous dinner at the King's Head Inn. The whole passed off without the least disturbance.'

The lack of disturbance probably meant that the Gloucestershire constabulary were out in force. Samuel Rudder, the local historian half a century earlier, had been greatly troubled by the violence which accompanied these phoney elections, and recognised the cause. But the *Standard*, which had been founded to combat 'the fierce spirit of a licentious Democracy' and which had denounced the proposed secret ballot as 'unmanly and un-English' launched an effective smear-campaign against one of the few signs of organised labour in the district: the Working Man's Association.

'The unwashed inhabitants of this town have recently established a Club . . . which is held at the Salutation Inn, in Cricklade Street', the paper reported in November 1837. 'The members have gotten up a petition for Universal Suffrage, which, after being hawked about to every pot-house, and the houses of every dirty alley in the town and neighbourhood, has, as near as we could see (which was no very easy matter in consequence of its dark and greasy appearance,) about 300 names affixed to it, of which nine-tenths are probably boys or non-electors.' In spite of its snobbishness the paper saw fit to report in detail on the ensuing gatherings of chimney-sweeps, painters, 'horse-clippers' and the like in order to name names, emphasise the inflammatory and possibly treasonable nature of the proceedings, and terrorise tradesmen afraid of losing their custom into publicly dissociating themselves from the organisation. J. Angelo of Cricklade Street wrote to the *Standard* to protest that he was no horse-clipper, that he had nothing to do with the Working Man's Association, and that 'it would enjur me in my buisniss as a hair dresser and Perfumer' if people thought that he did. The newspaper gleefully published the letter with all the spelling mistakes left in as part of its campaign of denigration and ridicule.

It is difficult today to imagine Cirencester as a ferment of working-class radicalism. In fact the unrest died away as the hungry forties gave way to the more prosperous fifties, and by the time Richard Jefferies was working as a reporter on the *Standard* he found Cirencester, or Fleeceborough, as he called it in *Hodge and his Masters*, a prosperous town contented to be ruled by a landlord so wealthy that he could afford to be benevolent. The very vastness of his fortune assured the town under his protection a certain stability.

13

WE came back to London, briefly, during the summer holidays. It was odd to come back to the small flat as a visitor. My tiny room overlooking the concrete yard and the row of garages had been let to a schoolteacher, but since she had gone home to her native Wales I could sleep in my own bed. This wartime lodger decided my future: there was no question that when I passed my eleven-plus I would go on to the school where she taught geography.

Even after she moved on to larger lodgings she kept in touch, sent me birthday cards, came for tea in fluffy pastel jumpers and chiffon scarves which looked odd on her stout figure. There was never any doubt in my mother's mind that her recommendation of the grammar school in which she worked was more than enough in choosing a school for me. And, being a child, I was proud, as a first-former, to have a family friend on the staff.

My first glimpse of her was unforbidding. She was indulgently kind to small children, smiled a lot, and sniffed through her nose when she laughed. Pretty features in a middle-aged face, a heavy woman with a taste for feminine frippery.

London was much quieter now. We played on the grass verge, thick with wild peppermint, of our jerry-built medieval castle, finished just before the outbreak of war. It was genuine enough in some ways: odd shaped rooms, no flat with the same layout, not a single window with a normal vista. They all looked either on to the concrete courtyard with its line of garages or on to a piece of embattled wall. And the plumbing was in tune with the spirit of the age: each winter the pipes froze, then burst, and the flat was laid out with buckets and bowls placed at strategic points to catch the drips. My brother slept in the dining-room with an umbrella above his pillow.

After a couple of winters my mother had had enough. Her terror of mice was probably the decisive factor. One could hear them scuttling in the ceiling overhead, and we were warned of the dire consequences of allowing crumbs of food to fall on the floor: a mouse invasion. I puzzled my head about how mice could get down through the apparently impenetrable ceilings, but I was assured that mice had ways and means of getting in anywhere. In 1942 we moved down the road to a more solid block of flats. It was noisier, with much more traffic, including buses, passing outside. Once the onslaught of flying bombs and rockets began it was even less quiet, but the building was solid enough to withstand both blast and heavy vibration.

'Reinforced concrete', our night visitors would reassure each other, murmuring the words like some magic spell of protection as the guns thundered, the night shook, and explosions followed in rapid succession. But flying bombs came by day as well as night, and without warning. By 1944 the reinforced concrete block had become little more than a ghost town, with most of the flats empty. It was the time when nerves began to fray, visibly. Even mine. Once I had sneaked off to school after an air raid warning when my mother's back was turned. I liked my new grammar school. In the first form we had taken end-of-term examinations with a prefect keeping watch on the school roof. When the whistle blew we got under the desks and took the opportunity to compare answers. But since I had mistaken the sound of a V1 for a 52 bus, scoffed at my mother's warning and been caught, seconds later, in a terrifying blast which shattered every shop window across the road and sucked out my guts together with our net curtains through closed windows, I had become a nervous child who took shelter before she was told, who retired to the hallway with a book under one arm and a cushion under the other at the least ominous sound.

But that was still to come. In the summer holiday of 1941 we played peacefully enough on the top of our suburban hill crowned with its three fake castles where four roads met. We played cowboys and Indians at the foot of turrets with slit windows, ran along walls and up crazy stone stairways chasing each other, and somehow as a girl I was always an Indian being shot at by boys who had the guns, trying to find a place to hide. And we sat in my dolls' cot and rolled down the hill on it. At the bottom of the hill we met other kids on what had once been the village green. Now it housed a bus shelter backed by a public lavatory. Main roads made up two sides of the old triangle, with bus stops on both of them. At the north end was the blue police box and the high mast of the air-raid siren. When you saw the bobby on duty move from the telephone to the siren we knew it was time to break up the game and go home.

Other things were still to come. The identity that Isolde had planted on me so bewilderingly one night in the dormitory, that strange word 'Jewish', was to acquire less mystery and a terrible reality. Unnamed tensions attached themselves to this state of being, of things unsaid, hinted at, a dark horror at the heart of the family which could not be spoken about but brooded over the dining table, turned small disputes about everyday trifles into momentous schisms, minor scratches into gaping, gangrenous wounds that required a sort of amputation. But the dark mystery which Isolde had first invoked remained, because I still did not know just how much was involved in the words that I did hear. I knew that my grandparents had been 'deported', for instance, by the time I had passed my eleven-plus and become a first-former at the local grammar school, but I did not know all that the word implied, and it was not something one could ask questions about at home. And I felt that adults were themselves groping at a dark heart of half-understood horrors, where reluctance to come to terms with the probable was overshadowed by anxiety about the possible. There was also a wish to spare the children, not to become too explicit. But children cannot be spared. Instead of sharing the burden, they become its ignorant victims. When tension became too much and the storm finally broke, I found myself like a lightning conductor, suddenly charged with what for me became a guilt of horrendous proportions.

Now that I have been a mother myself, coping alone, I know

how easily unhappiness and anxiety which you are trying to keep to yourself can build up inside until one small annoyance, the irritating obstinacy of a child who dawdles, argues, or refuses to obey a simple request can be the last straw and unwittingly cause an outburst quite disproportionate to the offence. I also know that during those six years my mother was coping alone with stresses which my generation has not had to face. But I did not know it then; I only knew that I was a child living with a mother who often seemed harassed and preoccupied, so that I felt excluded, shut out, or unjustly persecuted.

And then the abnormalities of war seemed normal to me. I had grown up with them, they formed the daily background of my growing up, with its self-centred daydreams and ambitions. But one day there was yet another minor argument which flared up between us and my mother blurted out the truth: how could I be so difficult when she was worried out of her mind because her father and stepmother had been deported?

I was crushed. Appalled. I sat by myself in shame and misery, thinking: *why hadn't she told me?* I told myself it was unfair, how was I supposed to know, and at the same time I felt it was all my fault, her unhappiness, my unreasonableness, even the death of those I loved. From now on there was no escape from the burden of guilt.

My father's infrequent home leaves were spoiled for me in advance because, hardly had he come through the door and deposited his kitbag in the passage, taken off his heavy boots, hugged me in his rough, scratchy battledress and found some chocolate in his breast pocket, than he would be shut up in the bedroom with my mother and given a long account of my bad behaviour. I would listen to their voices through the wall, miserably certain that it was all about me. By now my brother had proved so unruly without a man in the house that he had been packed off to another boarding school and, frankly, I envied him. Considering that his own existence at that time was no picnic, my father would be remarkably understanding and patient. When he finally came out of the bedroom and into the living room, where I sat waiting for my turn, he was very gentle: 'Now try to understand. Your mother is having a very difficult time just now. You must try and help.' I protested that I did . . . but . . . but. But it was all too much for me.

The time came when I understood completely, and the last shadows of secrecy were torn away. One bright afternoon in early spring my mother gave me ninepence and sent me to the local cinema. 'Go and see,' she said. 'Go and see for yourself.' I sat alone in the dark cinema and watched the newsreel of Belsen: mounds of corpses, dazed survivors with huge haunted eyes staring out of skulls which had become too heavy for the frail emaciated bodies, mute evidence for the prosecution posing for the camera. At last I knew what it meant to be a Jew, the shameful secret which had been hinted at but kept from me for so many years, the mark on my head which I did not recognise but which Isolde had known about four years before, in the dormitory, when I was a small child, innocent as Eve in the Garden of Eden, and as ignorant.

In those days, in Cirencester, I did not know what it meant to belong to the human race. Now I knew. I was not a child any longer. I came out into the cold suburban sunshine, where the trees in the front gardens were just beginning to break into blossom, blinking in the sharp light after the cavernous dark of the cinema, mute, tearful, and stupefied. I walked down the road in my cotton socks and the child's gingham frock with the white collar. Underneath the straight gingham front my nipples had begun to swell painfully, like small hard boils.

We did not talk much at home. The subject was avoided. But I began to have a recurring dream, in which I regularly relived the moment of departure, the point of no return. The dream was faithful to reality: the plane waiting for take off on the tarmac of Berlin airport. And a row of abandoned loved ones standing outside the airport building, waving wistfully at survivors whom they could no longer see.

The dream recurred with great regularity all through my adolescence and into my early twenties. Having shrugged off my guilt as irrational, I thought nothing of it until one day, on a psychoanalyst's couch, I mentioned it in one of those awkward silences when one talks about last night's dream simply to get a sticky session moving. For something to say. I described the grey overcast day, sitting in the plane, watching my relatives through the window, tiny remote figures on the edge of the airfield. And instead of going on to discuss it I found myself, for the first and last time, crying uncontrollably and beyond words.

*　*　*

My other grandmother, a wealthy widow who, before the war, had lived in a vast apartment of gloomy splendour on the Kurfürstendamm, managed to outwit the Germans. We heard that she was still alive from an elderly woman who managed to get herself 'exchanged' very late in the war: she was Jewish, but had British nationality because she was the widow of a man, dead for decades, who had left England at the age of two. Frau Landsberg had become a friend of my grandmother, who was living in hiding and was, it seemed, planning to buy her way out of Germany together with a number of other wealthy Jews. We heard the story, and my parents were sceptical, the plan seemed so far-fetched and unlikely. A Swiss bank was involved, and the deal was for the group of Jews to buy a shoe factory in Guatemala from a Nazi who wanted to return to the fatherland in its hour of need, in return for safe conduct to a neutral country. Months went by. We had never even started to hope. The summer of 1944 arrived, my father came home on leave, embarkation leave before being shipped to Normandy, though he kept that little detail to himself. He was shaving in the bathroom, stripped to the waist, when the telegram arrived. His mother was in Stockholm. We gathered in the bathroom, hugged and kissed my father's soapy, half-shaved face as he sat on the edge of the bath, smiling but half dazed.

That was June 1944. By September, prematurely aged from the years in hiding, her heart worn out, she was dead. My father was away in France. We had exchanged a few letters. I looked forward to having a grandmother of my very own once the war was over. I felt cheated by her death, but I also felt a guilt which I carefully kept to myself. In one of my letters I had told her of my outrageous and daring plan: I intended to go on the stage. Actresses were not respectable: I felt guiltily convinced that the shock of having a granddaughter on the stage had been too much for her.

I never really knew her. I had an image of a grand old lady, imperious as a dowager duchess, with a chauffeur-driven limousine and an apparent immunity to the charms of small children, whose whims were strictly subordinated to her personal routine. She was capable of ignoring me altogether while she ate pineapple and a boiled egg for breakfast, and I fidgeted in a chair opposite her, licking salt. And when I told her that she snored as she took her afternoon nap in the room next to mine I was quite disgraced for a while.

I never really knew her, except through the eyes of a very small child, and the image I had was not very favourable. One of the rewards of this book has been to find something of her more than thirty years after her death, a touch of the real human being. Checking on dates, my mother told me that she still had those few letters she wrote between her escape and death. They are heart-rending in their longing, gratitude, and humility. She hoped my father had forgiven her for making life more difficult for him through her own shortsightedness, for not seeing things as they were until it was too late. She wrote of her dreadful fears for her daughter Margot, who had moved with her husband and children to Paris in 1933 and gone underground in the Dordogne after the German invasion. By the time my father had managed to reach Paris in his British army uniform and learnt from a suspicious concierge that his sister and her family were safe, my grandmother had died of heart failure. There was a letter to me and my brother. She longed to know how much we had grown, whether we had changed out of all recognition. Each time she wrote she begged for photographs of us, and never got them, because of wartime censorship.

The war, and our situation, would unfold and grow in dimension as I grew older in understanding and left the best years of my childhood behind. I spent the latter years of the war looking forward to that unimaginable time of bliss, known as Peacetime, or When the War is Over. None of us kids were old enough to have any clear conception of what such a time could be like, and we looked forward to it as something remote, not understood, but blissful, like faithful Christians thinking about the rewards of an afterlife in heaven. Sweet rationing would stop.

I was old enough to share in the excitement of D-Day, which at long last signified the beginning of the end. A first-former now, at the local grammar school, I walked home one sunny June afternoon: every window was open, and from every window came the sound of the wireless giving the latest news from the front. Next day at school we all drew a map of Europe in our exercise books and, starting with a tiny red blotch at Caen, copied the line of the Allied advance from the blackboard each day. It was slow at first, but then our crayons took in broader and broader sweeps, until the speed of events made our exercise books look a mess and we gave up the project and waited for the inevitable end.

We had two days' school holiday. I stayed up half the night to watch the fireworks, the bonfires, and to join in the dancing with total strangers to music relayed on to the front lawn of the block of flats. My mother did not celebrate. She went to bed and smiled sadly when I came back indoors to tell her what was going on outside. I tried to persuade her to come out, but she was in no mood to celebrate.

And so the time that, as kids, we had tried so hard to imagine, had finally arrived. It was not much different from before, except in little ways. The heavens did not open, the skies were as grey as before, in spite of Vera Lynn. And sweets were still strictly rationed.

But in the summer of 1941 all this was still in the future. I was aged nine, I was going back to Cirencester after the holiday, and a vestige of magic, of a childhood paradise, still clung to my existence.

14

All I remember about coming back was my mother taking us for lunch on the first floor of Viner's which then, as now, occupied two floors in Castle Street near the Market Place. 'You'd better eat as much as you can', she said in a matter-of-fact tone, like a general preparing his troops for a long winter campaign. I stared out of the window and thought about going back, looking down at houses and streets and stonework which had become so familiar, with the inevitability of the everyday. Round the corner in Lewis Lane the spare old house with its many echoing rooms, bare floors, rather cold, would be waiting for me. Zoë, brisk of manner but loving, beaked nose and humour lines etched round her eyes, and her no-nonsense-you're-not-babies way of talking, would be expecting us. If I wanted to go back, this reminder of daily gnawing hunger had a dampening effect. We had been eating as much as we could, my brother and I, throughout the holidays. We found it an odd experience: now and again we would look at each other and exchange rather sheepish grins, compounded of disbelief not unmixed with a touch of guilt, as we made pigs of ourselves, thus Zoë would have put it, by eating until we had had enough. My mother only had to utter a simple 'Would you like some more?' for our eyes to widen in amazement. We would exchange glances, giggle in nervous incredulity before we learned to relax and make the most of our chance. The tiny larder was like an Aladdin's cave capable of satisfying our most unreasonable wishes. But now we were back on the verge of reality.

So we fortified ourselves with a final lunch at Viner's, which seemed to me then the last word in sophisticated high living for some reason. Perhaps because the rooms were light and airy, and downstairs fancy cakes were displayed on glass shelves. It must have been the modernity: most of the inns and tea-rooms in the town were darkish places, with little parchment-shaded lamps, tables and chairs of stained wood in Windsor style, and low ceilings with oak beams. The floors and walls were often uneven, tapering off to dark corners where you sat hidden from the rest of the room. But here we sat in light and airy splendour, with the town spread out below. I felt that my mother had somehow staked everything on this last lunch together. I tried to do justice to the occasion, but after several weeks in London I had stopped being ravenous. Alas, human beings cannot store up food in advance. I knew that a week from now I would think back to this meal with regret. But even so, I could not manage a second helping.

The images of that last term are of winter closing in, days growing shorter. The mournful smell of mist and damp leaves turning to rot, it hung in the garden, in the park, it seeped into the stonework of the house and clung to the damp basement, so we shivered if we had to go to the lavatory first thing in the morning when thick white air curled in through the black iron railings of the area gate. The lime tree turned yellow and dropped dead leaves on to the damp lawn. Soon it became too cold to spend our break between lessons outside. Occasionally we took a quick look at the rabbits huddled in their hutches, then abandoned them to the cold, quivering with pink eyes and rheumy noses in their fur coats. Somebody would be sent out with a bucket to feed the chickens. In the abandoned kitchen garden the beehive had stopped humming.

On our free afternoons we went to the park and shuffled through the fallen leaves under the ancient trees, searching for beechnuts which complimented our meagre diet, picking up chestnuts and pine cones to take back. The shadows would be closing in now, quite fast, as we passed through the high iron gates beside the Armoury and walked down Cecily Hill and through the narrow winding streets. Bats wheeled and screeched like wild black leaves high above the giant yew hedge at the main gate to Cirencester House, barely visible against the faintly luminous dark night sky. We stopped to watch them, and told each other, in some awe, about how bats could get caught in your hair, which meant having it all cut off. Wide-eyed, shuddering with not unpleasurable horror, we filed on past the museum and walked towards the Market Place, through the winding narrow streets, back home.

Tea in the long room overlooking the garden now already swallowed up by the night. A coal fire burning in the grate. Perhaps Miss Betts, her ostrich features and long legs relaxed now, mellowed by lamplight and fireglow, would read us a story before it was time to go up to bed. Or we would stand round the fireplace until fingers and toes thawed out and tingled, making chilblains a certainty. Occasionally we roasted chestnuts, waiting for them to pop and explode on the grate. And on hairwash nights I squatted alone in front of the fire, the room empty and in shadow, until it was dry. My hair was considered something of a problem, too thin and silky, pigtails which were mere wisps. Zoë and Hillie's remedy was probably Victorian, and consisted of regularly singeing the ends. The potent smell of burning hair clung to that schoolroom and fireside for all time. As a reward for being brave during this nerve-racking ordeal Hillie heated a pair of curling tongs in the fire and produced locks and ringlets on my head as if by magic.

The winter closed in. My brother's face looked miserable and sickly. He did not whine, but looked at me reproachfully. Zoë marched him off to see a doctor, but in spite of the prescribed ultra-violet treatment, the spoonfuls of cod liver oil and malt from the big jar in the scullery, he stayed whey-faced and listless.

My mother came to take him home. I had been stitching a traycloth, the first of many, for her birthday: Miss Betts taught me lazy daisy, stem stitch and an edging of blanket stitches. I apologised for not having it ready on time, and found out that I had muddled her birthday in November with her wedding anniversary which had come and gone in September. So I went back and filled in all the lazy daisies on the transfer and sent if off in good time for the first of many Novembers. Each year the cloths got bigger, the stitches finer and more

137

ambitious. Neat daughterly duty, carefully stitched, from blue transfer patterns.

My brother gone, I was left behind in the old house with its large echoing rooms, winter air seeping in from attic schoolroom to basement scullery. The mornings were dark now, it was hard to get out of the narrow iron bed with its rough grey blankets, army style, now that the air was shivering cold. The room, like the long schoolroom below, had a fireplace, but this one was never lit. We were provided with stone hot-water bottles and took to slipping into bed in our underclothes, vests, liberty bodices, and navy blue knickers. Lying in bed, I rubbed at my itching swollen fingers and feet until the chilblains broke and Zoë came with ointment and bandages. My sufferings were rewarded by being excused piano practice, since nobody could be expected to play properly with a bunch of swollen reddish purple sausages. For me it was a relief not to be expected to play properly, since the tension and anxiety associated with my piano lessons from Zoë had never entirely subsided, and I was dreadfully conscious of my own inadequacy.

But even the hardships of school life had by now become so familiar that I took them in my stride as something normal. Bare floorboards, shared baths, the damp lavatory in the basement with squares of old newspaper in the lavatory paper holder, these were simply aspects of a way of life which had become mine: the normal everyday flavour of a cosmos infinitely rich and strange, a household ruled by two spinster sisters who were constantly opening doors behind which lay untold riches; songs, stories, books, legends, walking, memories caught in a sepia photograph, hedgerows filled with history, the flotsam of a world as miraculous as dandelion clocks blown into the wind. Even the door to my remote childhood had been unlocked when, in a singing session round the piano, Zoë asked me to sing a song because it was in German, and by Schubert, and a childhood dream of a youth in fancy dress who picked a wild rose and put it in a box suddenly found its source.

Food continued to be an obsession, but it had been going on so long that my body had adjusted. The raw, desperate edge went out of the gnawing hunger. I found comfort in the lumps of sugar or cheese which Zoë sometimes handed round just before bedtime, the burnt toast from the teacher's table, and any other scraps which came my way by whim or chance. And by now I knew myself to be a survivor: it was my brother who had succumbed and gone home. I knew, my mother knew, that all he needed to get well was more food. I felt sorry for him, but no envy. I was too busy opening doors: reading books, looking and listening, dreaming, fumbling for words and arranging them on a page, and finding me, a person in my own right, with eyes that could see, ears listen, mind master and think and put words together and respond to the kindness and expectation of people who did not claim ownership over me but saw me as me, someone unique and individual of whom much could be expected. A child whose needs were amply catered for, including wintergreen for chilblains, and hair singed in front of a glowing coal fire.

* * *

One dark winter morning in December I was woken at five o'clock to catch the train for London. I was going home for Christmas. Miss Betts accompanied me and my small suitcase. I remember shivering on a bleak railway platform in the half-light, waiting for the train to come in. We got out at Swindon, where I was put in charge of a nun I had never seen before. She was escorting several schoolgirls back to London, and I made one more. Nobody said much on the journey in the overcrowded carriage, which had the bizarre quality of a dream in my tired fuddled state. I felt an outsider, a parcel unceremoniously dumped on people I did not know, but the nun was kind enough, and seemed quite like a normal human being, in spite of her odd clothes.

I was going home just for the Christmas holiday. Woken in the early hours of the morning, when it was dark and cold and I was dazed with lack of sleep, I had hardly spoken to anyone. A few brief words with Zoë, but no goodbye. It would only be for a few days anyhow. My mother waited until we were back in the flat and I had taken my outdoor clothes off. 'I've got a surprise for you,' she said. I waited. Christmas was the time of

139

year for surprises, good things. 'I've got a surprise for you. You're not going back after Christmas.'

The shock left me speechless. A trick had been played on me. 'I didn't want to tell you before but . . .' So Zoë had also been tricked: she did not know, any more than I did. 'The bombing is not so bad now so . . .' My misery was boundless, it welled up like a sea and threatened to engulf me, trickle out of my eyes, gush out of my mouth. But I knew there was nothing I could say. She was waiting for me to look pleased. She was pleased. I managed to hold in the tears, hold in my misery, but not much more. I do not think she noticed, since she took it for granted that I would want to be home for good. It was only natural where a child was concerned. I tried hard to behave naturally, as though nothing had happened to me. But the gates of my happy childhood had clanged shut behind me; I had become adult enough to recognise the need to conceal unbearable emotions for the sake of others. In their own way the two sisters had prepared me for life after the inevitable expulsion.